TAKING STUDENTS ABROAD

A Complete Guide for Teachers

MAGGIE BROWN CASSIDY

with illustrations by Robert MacLean

PRO LINGUA ASSOCIATES

Published by Pro Lingua Associates
15 Elm Street
Brattleboro, Vermont 05301

802-257-7779
SAN 216-0579

This 1988 edition of **Taking Students Abroad** is a revision of an earlier edition published by J. Weston Walch, publisher, of Portland, Maine; copyright © 1984. The author and the publisher of this revision appreciate the cooperation of the original publisher.

ISBN 0-86647-028-X

Printed in the United States of America.

Contents

9 Get Ready—Orientation   83

10 Get Set—   105

DEDICATION

This book is for Brownie and Kitty, who helped me start traveling; for Dan, who helps me keep going; and for my students: traveling with them is a privilege and a pleasure.

ACKNOWLEDGEMENTS

This book grew out of two exchanges between Brattleboro Union High School and schools in Geneva, Switzerland. I learned by doing, and many people helped along the way. I would like to thank the following people and institutions for all their help:

Al Lynch, former chairman of the language department at B.U.H.S., who has generously encouraged me at every step, both with the exchanges and with the book itself:

Tony Broom, principal, and the school board of B.U.H.S., who supported both exchanges and granted me a leave of absence to work on the book;

Bernard Troesch and John Ankers, who organized the Swiss side of our exchanges and helped me organize the American side;

Skip and Ginger Gordon, who led the parents' group in both exchanges. Their enthusiasm and hard work could move mountains, and many of the fund-raising and public relations ideas came from them;

Ann Cummings, Sue Haskins, Janette Neubauer, and Marion Holway, who shared their experiences and concerns as parents of students in the exchanges;

Mary Ellen Anderson, Rocky Ravenna, Pat Murphy, Calico Harington, Marge Yoder, Jeff Record, Jenny Stone, Lisa Neubauer, Carroll Cummings, Jenny Callahan, Carrie Webster, Melissa Howe, John Todd, Mary Ellen Reuter, Ted Soulos, Melissa Mann, Kathy Long, Sue Detch, Deirdre Baker, Doug Jefferson, and Andrea Gordon, students whose experiences contributed directly to this book;

The Dartmouth Humanities Institute, and particularly Bob Williams, whose active listening helped me get started writing;

Diane Fagin-Adler, whose support as Foreign Language Consultant for the State of Vermont helped at several points along the way;

The Experiment in International Living, for allowing me to print an adaptation of its evaluation form;

The Ibero-American Cultural Exchange Program, for allowing me to reprint its cross-cultural observation guide;

Professor J. Doyle Casteel and his colleagues at the Center for Latin American Studies at the University of Florida at Gainesville, for allowing me to print an adaptation of a role-play;

Gary Adamsky, of Montpelier High School, for sharing his fund-raising ideas with me;

Charlie Andromidas of Youth for Understanding, who helped invent some of the role-plays described in Chapter 9;

Gordon Hayward, who gave my students guidance and inspiration for keeping journals, and helped me revise the manuscript;

Bob Schermer, German teacher at South Burlington High School, who suggested having students present projects while they're abroad;

Leslie Friend, whose packing list I adapted;

Jenny Brown, who helped me figure out what teachers leading students abroad might want to know, and whose orientation schedule is included here;

Sue Chilson, who shared her ideas and materials on student travel;

Karen Libby, who helped devise various forms and orientation activities and shared the leadership of one exchange;

Howie Shapiro, who shared crosscultural materials with me;

Linda Dempsey, who shared some information about electrical matters;

Margie Wilson, who helped with the typescript;

and finally, Dan, my husband, whose constant support and encouragement made this book possible.

Introduction

A trip to another country offers students extraordinary opportunities to learn—about the new country, their own culture, and themselves. Unfortunately, many student groups travel abroad without ever really leaving home: they rush from one tourist attraction to another by charter bus, escorted by guides assigned to them; they eat only familiar foods; and the only people they deal with are professionals in tourism who have no time for individuals.

Bringing students into contact with another culture isn't easy. Lots of organizations and companies exist to serve groups of students who are willing to travel *en masse,* but very few exist to serve groups who want to get off the beaten path; the teacher ends up doing a lot of work arranging the trip. I hope this book will help teachers ask the right questions as they plan their students' trip.

Students themselves often resist confronting a new culture, since they're often unsure of themselves even in familiar situations and don't like to risk being misunderstood or laughed at or ignored. If they're to overcome this natural reluctance, they'll have to begin preparing for the trip long before they leave: they must see that they will be able to survive— on their own—in a new culture, and perhaps in a new language. I believe that how students prepare themselves for a trip determines what their experience will be. Group activities— fund raising and public relations as well as actual orientation—should help the students build their sensitivity to a new culture, their sense of responsibility to the group, and their self-confidence. In this book I've devoted more space to preparation and follow-up than to the trip itself, because I believe that the teacher's role is to prepare the students and structure their experience and then stand by as they go through it. When students are ready to meet the challenges of foreign travel, their self-reliance and self-confidence grow because they test themselves in each new situation. A well-planned trip can provide so many challenges each day—from taking the bus to trying new foods to fitting into a new family—that students grow and change literally from one day to the next. No other teaching situation is so satisfying to me as sharing that intense experience with my students and watching them grow.

Taking Students Abroad is arranged in chronological order, from the initial planning of a trip through forming a group, fund raising and orientation, to the trip itself, and follow-up. The examples come from trips to Mexico and Europe because I have first- or second-hand experience with those areas, but I hope most of the information and suggestions will be useful for travel to other regions, too.

If you're thinking of taking a group of students abroad, I suggest that you skim through the whole book, noting things you may want to come back to later, as the trip progresses from idea to reality. The ideas and suggestions have worked either for me or for colleagues in Vermont; you'll want to adapt them to your own situation. It's also helpful to keep a loose-leaf notebook for copies of memos, letters, orientation materials, the minutes of your group's meetings, and lists.

Bon voyage!

—Maggie Brown Cassidy

1

Think It Over

Why do you want to take students abroad?

If you take a few minutes to think about why you want to take your students traveling, you can answer a lot of other important questions about the trip at the same time. If your trip is based on some activity (the chorus is going to sing in a concert tour; the drama club is going to see plays; the soccer team has a series of matches), obviously other aspects of the trip will fall into place around these activities. Or if your main goal is simply for your students to see the sights, and you're not concerned about putting them in touch with people in the country you want to visit, a package tour might be the easiest and least expensive way to go.

Perhaps you have different reasons for wanting to travel with your students. Maybe you want your students to have a chance to get to know people their own age who live in another country; maybe you want your students to be surrounded by the language they've been learning, so they can improve the communicative skills they've been working on in your foreign-language class—and bring their new skills and enthusiasm back to share with other students. Maybe you want them to develop the confidence and self-reliance that come with testing oneself against the daily challenges of travel abroad.

You probably want to go for yourself, too. You will get to share the students' experiences as they confront those challenges. At the same time, you, too, can immerse yourself in the whole experience, broadening and updating your knowledge of the language and culture; you can bring back videotapes, realia, slides, taped interviews.

If your goal is to engage your students with the host country's language and culture, you must plan the whole trip with that goal in mind. Every aspect of the experience, from recruiting through preparation to follow-up, should encourage the students to explore the language and culture, to work together, and to take responsibility for what they are learning. They'll need a lot of help from you, since for most of them this trip will be a first experience abroad—at least, a first experience of this kind. They won't know what to expect, much less how to react appropriately to it. I find it helpful to think of myself as a coach, working with the students to prepare them. For this reason, most of these pages are about preparation, with a few about follow-up and only a very few about the actual travel: if the preparation is adequate, there will be nothing left to do during the trip itself but to experience and enjoy it.

There are long-term rewards as well as immediate ones. In 1981 a boy I'll call Mike was a participant in our exchange. Mike was a senior; he was interested in becoming a lawyer and seemed to have no ear for French at all. During the trip to Switzerland, he picked up "souvenirs" from our hotel in Paris and various cafes; the last straw came when he pocketed a wine-glass from the *cave* that had given us a tour and a wine-tasting. On our return to school, he seemed to lose whatever motivation he had had to learn French; as I remember, he dozed through the spring-semester course. The Swiss students visited that summer. Mike was Mr. Hospitality, a side of him I had never seen: he took part in every activity and tirelessly chauffeured them around in his VW. When he went off to the University of Vermont, I thought I would never see him again.

To my astonishment, he tracked me down at a conference at the University a year later, and asked me for a recommendation for UVM's junior-year-abroad program in Nice.

"I know we had our problems during the exchange," he said, "and I wasn't exactly your star pupil—but I'm really interested in French and I'd like to go on this program. I'll be able to take political science courses—all in French—at the University of Nice." So I wrote a recommendation, tactfully stressing how much he had contributed to the American side of our exchange.

He wrote me a letter in impeccable French from Nice, raving about his wonderful year there. Then he stopped in at school after he had graduated from UVM. He told me—in only slightly accented French—that he had joined the Peace Corps, and would be leaving soon for Cameroon. And then, in 1987, on leave from the Peace Corps, he came to my classes to show slides of the Cameroon, and to narrate in French (with traces of an African lilt). My students thought he was exotic and wonderful; they could hardly believe that he had been a student like themselves. I wanted to say to them, "*This* is what can happen once you start to travel."

Why do your students want to go?

Ask them. Most of them will tell you whatever they think you want to hear—that they want to use their German, or that they want to meet a Mexican family. They may be sincere; they may also have other reasons to travel, as you'll find out if you listen to them talk to each other. They want to be with their friends. They want to drink (the giveaway to this is when they ask you, "Is it true there's no drinking age in _____?"). They want to get away from their parents, or they want to buy things to impress their friends. Probably few will be as ingenuous as one of my students who announced that he was going to England with the school trip next year and would be needing my recommendation. When I asked why he wanted to go to England, he shrugged. "I don't know," he said. "Just someplace to go, I guess."

All these desires—including the desire just to go someplace—are perfectly natural. Some of them may run directly counter to your goals for your students: if they spend most of their time drinking with their friends, they won't be able to get very involved with the new culture. If any students are really unwilling or unable to subordinate their immediate goals to the group's educational purposes, you should become aware of that fact, so you can tactfully ease them out of the group as soon as possible.

In most cases you can help the students put their individual desires into perspective and add some other, more educational goals to their reasons for going. For example, students might not realize how much responsibility and freedom they will have during their time abroad; most begin to grow into that responsibility immediately as they begin to understand it and prepare for it. For another example, it might not occur to most adolescents that they can make real, lasting friendships with someone they meet in another country. Two of the students who went on our first exchange, in 1979, went to Switzerland to visit their counterparts nine years later; in 1986 Mike's Swiss partner in the 1981 exchange visited him for a month in Africa. When they were in high school, probably none of those young people imagined that as adults they would remain friends with their counterparts.

A homestay

I'm convinced that the best way for students to see what it's like to live in another country is to live with a family. They use the new language, or at the very least they are surrounded by it 24 hours a day; they see first-hand the occupations and preoccupations of the country's ordinary citizens; they eat their food, at whatever hour it is normally eaten; in short, they plunge willy-nilly into the culture, and deal with it.

A homestay, by separating students from other members of the group, forces them to get involved with host nationals simply to survive. They can't take refuge in the group, relying on Mary Ellen to order lunch or Jeff to buy their stamps. They must answer questions ranging from, "Did you sleep well?" to "What do you think of our country?"

In the midst of this constant participation in family life, students can hardly help establishing close relationships with their host families; they begin to feel that, for better or for worse, they belong to those families. At the same time, when students in the group share their experiences, they discover lots of variety among their families, and they realize that no particular family is The Typical Family of that country.

A homestay not only gives each American a family, but it also gives each family an American. Each student is *the* foreign guest in that family, and all the pleasures and challenges of that role are the student's alone. The family will ask why Americans do things this way or think that way. For most students the role of spokesperson and representative of the American way of life is a new one—after all, it's the life they've always known. The students' discovery is thus doubled: at the same time that they're trying to understand a new culture, they're helping other people understand theirs. Both activities provide a deeper understanding of the American culture they've always taken for granted.

Of course, the success of a homestay depends on the attitude of everyone involved. It demands commitment: the students must be willing to give of themselves and not merely take in impressions as tourists do. It demands preparation: your students will have fears and hesitations about living with a family, and you will have to help them overcome these obstacles so that they can make the most of the experience. Most of all it demands flexibility and a sense of humor.

Nonprofit organizations exist to arrange homestay experiences for American students abroad. The best-known of these are the American Field Service, Youth for Understanding, and the Experiment in International Living. AFS has summer programs and full-year programs for individual students, and YFU has half-year and full-year programs for individual students. I especially recommend the Experiment, which arranges programs of varying length for both individual students and school programs.

AFS American Abroad Program
313 East 43rd Street
New York, NY 10017

The Experiment in International Living
Kipling Road
Brattleboro, VT 05301

Ibero-American Cultural Exchange Program   Nacel Cultural Exchanges
13920 93rd Avenue Northeast   Board of Trade Building #528
Kirkland, WA 98033   301 W. First Street
                                                    Duluth, Minn. 55802

Youth for Understanding
2501 Neward Street N.W.
Washington, DC 20016

The Ibero-American Cultural Exchange Program organizes six-week stays for high school students (both individuals and groups) in Mexico and a few Central American countries. The program begins with a six-day orientation, and then the students spend the rest of the time with a host family. Because the homestays are relatively long, students must be mature, flexible, and willing to adapt to a new way of life in order to understand it. For students who have those qualities, this remarkably inexpensive program is a wonderful opportunity to learn Spanish and live in a Spanish-speaking culture.

Nacel arranges four-week summer homestays in France for American students and similar experiences in the U.S. for French students. It also looks for interested teachers to lead the American groups. My students, who have both hosted and gone to France with this organization, have had wonderful experiences, and the cost is very reasonable. The program works through area coordinators; you can get the name of the person in your area by writing to the address above.

You may prefer to arrange the trip and the homestay yourself, even though doing so will mean extra time and work for you. First of all, the trip will cost the students less: you can work with a travel agent, so there are no middlemen, no matter how benevolent they may be. You and the travel agent will be doing the administrative work for which someone else would have to be paid. Eliminating those administrative costs brings the trip within the reach of almost any student who is willing to work hard to pay for it.

Secondly, if you arrange the homestay, you communicate directly with your counterpart in the other country. With that person's help you can prepare your students for their experience there and help them make the most of it.

Exchanges

Exchanges provide benefits over and above those of a simple homestay. Students will understand without having to be told that their trip isn't just a vacation, because the relationship they form with their counterparts must last over time and in two countries, in their hometowns among their families and friends as well as abroad. Because an exchange lasts longer and involves two sets of families, it demands more commitment from the students and families on both sides, and it's therefore more rewarding for all of them.

Exchanges can involve a whole community and can build support for the school and its programs. Community support sometimes pays off not only in goodwill, but also in hard cash: some merchants, companies, and community groups are much more willing to donate to an exchange, whose benefits they can see, than to a "mere" trip, which they may see as reserved for privileged students. They are often particularly willing to donate goods and services in order to make foreign visitors welcome in the community.

Finally, an exchange is the least expensive way for students on both sides to see each others' countries, since families take care of their guests' room and board (and sometimes other day-to-day expenses as well). If you and your group go directly to your homestay community and stay there, you can limit the out-of-pocket cost of the exchange to international travel, insurance, and spending money, plus activities that you plan for your guests when they come to you. Of course, if your group wants to travel on its own in addition to its homestay, the trip will cost more than a simple exchange, but the cost is still low compared with that of most tours.

The School Exchange Service, sponsored by the National Association of Secondary School Principals and the Council on International Educational Exchange, arranges exchanges between schools in the United States and similar schools in France, Germany, Britain, Spain, Japan, and Venezuela. In addition to pairing up schools, the School Exchange Service also arranges transportation, insurance, and in-country orientation. Its support services include regional meetings for program coordinators, guidelines and materials for selecting students, providing orientation, and planning programs for visitors.

I have no first-hand experience with this program, but its U.S. National Advisory Committee includes representatives from the American Council on the Teaching of Foreign Languages and various professional associations of language teachers, and its prices are reasonable. For more information, write to

> National Association of Secondary School Principals
> School Exchange Service
> 1904 Association Drive
> Reston, Virginia 22091

Package tours

If your students simply can't speak the language of the country they want to visit, a homestay would probably be too frustrating, both for them and for host families. There are still ways for them to see another country, however.

Brightly colored tour brochures stand out in the mountains of unsolicited mail that teachers receive. Amid pictures of smiling students in front of Notre Dame, the text offers you a free trip (and sometimes cash too, as competition in the industry gets fiercer) if you can recruit 10 or 15 students for a tour. The company offers to arrange all the details: insurance, transportation, hotels, some meals, sightseeing—leaving time, of course, for shopping. The packages are attractive because they cover a lot of ground, they're usually cheaper than custom-designed trips, and they save you, the teacher, a lot of time.

What are you giving up? Any chance for your students to learn self-reliance, and contact with the country you'll be visiting. The dilemma is purely economic: package-tour operators make money by dealing in volume. They need large groups in order to get discounts from airlines, hotels, restaurants, and tour guides. You may have only 10 students in your group, but you may find yourself traveling with five other groups at least as big. This one fact limits the kind of experience your students can have.

First of all, everyone will treat the group *as a group*. One of the rewards of international travel for students should be that they learn to be independent, to test themselves in new situations. Traveling in a huge mass defeats the purpose. A TWA employee at Logan Airport in Boston once told me, "You should have been here last night. It was crazy—there were so many student groups going to Europe that each leader had a different-colored flag.

The students had to look for the pink flag or the yellow flag." In such a situation, students are quick to lose themselves in the crowd; instead of taking on new responsibility, they become as dependent on their teacher as kindergarteners on a field trip to the post office. They understand that they don't have to make too many decisions, as long as they follow the pink flag.

It's hard for a crowd of Americans traveling together, no matter what their age, to see much of a country's daily life. After all, they spend most of their time together—in hotels, on chartered buses, on sightseeing tours. Because tour companies want to attract as many customers as possible, they aim for the lowest common denominator, following conventional tourist paths, choosing hotels that are as American as possible, serving safely American food. Travelers discover a new country when they are free to explore its side streets, talk with its people, and eat its food. They can't make those small but irreplaceable discoveries on a bus, or trudging around a monument.

And insurance? In general, tour companies seek to protect themselves, not you. In fact, many try to protect themselves *from* you, so that if anything goes wrong, you can't hold them liable. The Travel section of the *New York Times* reported (Sept. 6, 1981):

> Virtually every tour brochure contains a disclaimer of responsibility by the operator for almost everything a supplier of travel facilities might do wrong, whether consciously or as a result of force majeure.

Some companies that specialize in student travel do carry insurance for you, but be sure to read all the fine print. You may end up having to arrange for insurance coverage yourself; see "Insurance," Chapter 2.

If you decide to go with a package tour, ask the company to give you the name of a teacher near you who has taken one of its tours. You can ask that person for details about the tours and suggestions for preparing your students and making the most of that particular tour.

Trips you plan

You can avoid many of the drawbacks of a large commercial tour if you arrange your students' trip yourself. You eliminate middlemen (except your travel agent, who doesn't count, because his or her services don't directly affect the cost of the trip), so representatives of airlines, hotels, and other services will have a financial stake in pleasing you rather than a third party.

Working with an understanding travel agent (see "Find a travel agent," Chapter 2), you can design an imaginative and memorable tour for your students. Use your own interests and what you know about theirs to plan the outline of the trip: if you are a soccer fanatic, your students can learn a great deal about any country from watching a soccer match—and its audience. If some of your students like to act, you can plan to attend a play, or perhaps you could arrange to go backstage in a theater. If your students live in the city, they might like to spend some time in a small town, and vice versa. After students have signed up, you can incorporate their individual interests into the group, so that each of them will have a commitment to what the group is doing. You can also plan free time so that the group will be able to see the country at close range with the help of observation sheets and cross-cultural exercises.

Small-group tours are sometimes more expensive than package tours, but if you and the students plan it, the trip may be many times more interesting and valuable than a commercial tour could be. It's possible to keep the price low by finding small, inexpensive hotels and special fares and discounts; in order to take advantage of these discoveries, you'll need plenty of lead time.

In conclusion

I suspect that one reason teachers hesitate to organize trips themselves is that they dread the appalling amount of administrative work: keeping track of endless forms, sending out letters, typing and distributing lists, and supervising fund raising. Don't let the idea of all that work overwhelm you, because there's no reason you should do it all yourself. Call on the students and their parents. One student or one parent can take charge of each fund-raising activity; students or parents can type and run off handouts; students can help you distribute and collect forms.

Students' sharing the work is enormously helpful to you, of course, but it's also very important to them, though they may not realize it at the time. As with most things, what you get out of foreign travel depends almost entirely on what you put into it. Therefore, this book emphasizes planning and preparation, and the students should be involved in almost every aspect of those preparations. Certainly, you and the students could just pay some money to a tour company, meet once or twice, and then take off; lots of student groups do exactly that, and then they don't know why they feel vaguely disappointed by their experience. It stands to reason that you and your students will learn more and enjoy the trip more if you take the time to arrange a trip that suits you, to get to know one another, to learn something about the country you'll visit, and to prepare to immerse yourselves as deeply as you can in its daily life. There aren't many shortcuts in this preparation, but the work is more satisfying and fun when it's shared, and its rewards are the rich insights and friendships that a successful trip abroad can bring.

2

Set It Up

Get tentative approval from school authorities

After you've thought about why you'd like to take some students abroad, talk with people above you in the school's hierarchy. You will have to be rather vague about the details, but there's no use spending a lot of time setting up a trip for your students only to find out that the administrators or governing body of your school won't even consider the idea. To look at it more positively, encouragement from your administration will give you confidence to forge ahead. In sending out your inquiries, you can say, "We would like . . ." — and you can say it on school letterhead.

Lead time

Don't underestimate the time you'll need to arrange all the details of your trip. Just figuring out where to go, which students will go, and how much money you'll need, will take time— never mind raising money and preparing the students to get as much as they can out of the trip. If you and your students are planning a simple tour, allow six months' lead time; if you're looking for a homestay or an exchange, allow at least a year: it will probably take several months to find a counterpart across the border, and until you and that person are working together, the homestay is a wish and not a reality. If you already have a counterpart and know your destination, you can safely cut your lead time to six to eight months. They will be busy ones.

Planning for a year in advance may seem frustrating, since some of the students who are interested now may have graduated or lost interest in a year. It's still less painful to disappoint them and organize a successful trip for next year's students than to overreach yourself and have to skimp on necessary preparation or, worse yet, cancel the whole thing because you didn't allow enough time to work out the details.

Find a homestay community

Finding a community to welcome you will be easier than you may think. First, figure out where you'd be willing to go. For example, if you're a Spanish teacher, do you have to go to Spain? What about Mexico? The Spanish-speaking Caribbean islands? South America? Don't rule out places you've never been: though you'll have less specific information to share with your students, they'll see that you'll be learning with them, and that can be valuable, too.

Once you've decided, in a general way, where you want to go, cast your net as widely as possible: talk with your colleagues and friends; write to professional organizations (e.g., the National Council of Teachers of English, the American Association of Teachers of French). Often successful programs can expand, so if you hear of a group who has had a homestay in a country that interests you, get in touch with its leader and ask him or her for ideas. Call your state department of education, and try several different people there; even if the social studies specialist doesn't know of anything, the foreign language specialist might.

You can also focus on the foreign country itself: call or write the consulate of the country, or the cultural attaché at the country's embassy in Washington. If you'd like to focus on a relatively small area, you can write directly to schools in that area; if someone at the embassy or consulate doesn't have the appropriate addresses on hand, he or she can probably tell you how to obtain them. It was in just this way that my school's exchange with Switzerland began: one day our principal got a dittoed letter, addressed to all the high schools in Vermont, from someone named Bernard Troesch, a geography teacher in Geneva. He'd read about the canton's newly established sister-state relationship with the State of Vermont, and he wondered if any teachers in the state would be interested in setting up an exchange for our students. I was, and we did.

Your letter's tone is important because it represents you to people whom you've never met. Mr. Troesch's letter inspired confidence because it reflected his enthusiasm, his experience with student travel (he'd already organized exchanges between his students and students in England and Germany), and his willingness to be flexible about details of the exchange as we worked on it. When you write your letter, be specific about what you're looking for: Do you want to arrange homestays for your students? For how long? Are you interested in an exchange? If not, do the American students expect to welcome someone from their host family on a one-to-one basis? Can the students pay something toward their room and board? Do they want to be paying guests, or part of the family? Are they trying to learn the language? Is there a specific date when you want to go? Are some dates out of the question for you?

A delicate subject: very poor countries. If you're thinking of taking your students to a country whose students may not be able to afford to feed visitors, much less come to the United States, your letter should be that much more tactful. Don't assume that an exchange is impossible, since there may be resources that you don't know about; besides, hospitality is a very sensitive subject in most cultures. No matter what the other country's economic status, you should emphasize that your students are willing to live as ordinary people do—and then make sure they are.

Ask recipients of your letter to pass it along to someone else who may be interested if they're not. Don't be discouraged if you don't get a response right away. Cast your net more widely, talk to more people, and follow every lead. All you're looking for is one teacher who wants to work with you to make an opportunity for your—and that teacher's—students. There are plenty of people out there; don't give up the search.

You may get several responses. Choose the person who seems easiest for you to work with, since you'll be working closely with him or her. Thank the others, and if they're willing, pass their names on to other teachers in your area or to people in your state department of education or professional association. You may be able to spare another teacher all the groundwork you had to do.

How many stops will you make? In what order?

If your group is traveling for some specific purpose (to take part in concerts or athletic events, for example), your itinerary may already be set. If your trip includes a homestay, that will probably be the focus of your trip. Even if the main purpose of the trip is travel for its own sake, I suggest that you limit the number of stops to two for a 10-day tour, and two or three for a two-week trip. Everyone laughs at tours that try to cover seven European capitals in 10 days, but people still fall into that trap. You can see a lot more if you give yourself time to get acquainted with a place; rushing from city to city will begin to seem like a mobile slide-show.

Another suggestion: If your trip includes a stay in the country's capital or a main city, choose another, smaller, more typical place to visit as well. Too many Americans generalize about France and the French on the basis of their experiences in Paris, just as too many foreigners base their impressions of the U.S. on what they're seen of New York or Los Angeles. Which small city you choose will again depend on the students' interests and on your budget. They might be interested in visiting even a very small town indeed, if you can arrange accommodations and a variety of activities (some possibilities: renting bikes; hiking in mountains or along beaches; visiting a school; touring factories or farms). A bigger town may offer more variety, but the more cosmopolitan an area is, the less likely its people are to take time to get to know members of your group. In any case, you'd have to investigate what a given town has to offer before you settled on one; a travel agent could help you find the information you want. You may decide to offer your group two or three possibilities and ask them to choose one.

Whether or not your trip includes a homestay, I strongly recommend that you go to the big city *first:* the students can make their first adjustment to the new culture in a setting where people are used to foreigners. When the group arrives in a less touristy area, the students will be better prepared to focus on more subtle differences between the new area and their home. They'll be less likely to head for the nearest McDonald's and less shocked if they can't find one.

Another reason to put the city-stay first is that in doing so, you show your group that *you* are serious about seeing more than most tourists do. The students may be cool to the whole idea of going to a smaller town; it seems less glamorous than spending two weeks in Madrid or Mexico City, and it demands more from them. They may need to be persuaded that seeing a more typical, less tourist-oriented area is worthwhile and important; putting it late in the trip builds up its importance as well as their familiarity with the country and their ability to learn from such a visit. If they have a homestay, it's especially important that they don't think of it as just a necessary evil on the way to the excitement of the big city; if the city visit is behind them, there's no danger of their getting that impression—or, worse, of giving their host families that impression.

A final (and, to my mind, compelling) reason to put the city-stay first is that you'll have more control over the students while they're there. They'll be unsure of themselves at first, and they have a lot to lose if they misbehave. Later in the trip they'll have gained a lot of confidence (you may be amazed to see just how much), and they'll want to test their wings. The process will be easier on you, and safer for them, in a small city, where people know each other, than in a metropolis, where people are hardened to obnoxious or dangerous behavior.

Find a travel agent

A good travel agent can help you enormously as you plan your group's travel. He or she can not only arrange transportation for the lowest possible price, but also help you find hotels and things to do and see in a given place. It's much easier to work with one person than to deal with many different representatives of travel services, especially as the representatives are only voices on the phone or signatures on a letter. Best of all, the agent's services don't cost you or your group anything: his or her commission is included in the price of the airline ticket or hotel room. In effect every passenger pays a travel agent's commission, whether or not an agent handles the passenger's tickets and reservations—so why not use one?

Talk to several agents before you choose one. Since agents earn roughly 10% commission on their bookings, most will welcome your business. Try to find one who seems interested in what you're doing, eager to work with you, and willing to put up with the unavoidable penny-pinching and uncertainty that go along with student travel.

The more specific you can be about what you're looking for, the more help you can expect from the travel agent. At first you'll have only a general idea of what you'll need, but as the picture becomes clearer, be sure to stay in touch with the agent. He or she will need a lot of lead time to assure you of the routes and reservations you want, at the lowest possible price.

The Council on International Educational Exchange can help with some travel arrangements: among other things, it sponsors charter airline flights. To get detailed information about its services, write to:

> The Council on International Educational Exchange
> 205 East 42nd Street
> New York, New York 10017

Think About Basic Questions

Before you can begin to talk with students and organize a trip, you must think about the answers to the first questions they and their parents will ask. You may not yet have the answers to all of them; that's fine, as long as you have an idea when and how you'll get the answers.

Where are we going?

You may know only the country's name; you may already have a specific community as your destination.

Is this a school-sponsored trip?

Talk this question over with your administrators. They may not be able to give you a definite answer until the trip takes form, but they should be at least willing to consider the idea. This sponsorship can have any of the following implications for the trip:

- It shows that the school recognizes the educational value of the trip. It will be clear to everyone that the trip is an extension of your teaching duties, not a vacation for you or the students or a profit-making venture for you.

- The school may allow the students to miss some class time; it may even grant academic credit to students who go on the trip.

- The school may pay for a substitute teacher to replace you while the group is abroad, as it would pay for a substitute if you went on a one-day field trip.

- The school may have liability insurance for you, which would cover you in carrying out your duties as trip leader. It may, however, need an international rider (see "Insurance," this chapter).

- You can freely use the school's materials and facilities as you work with the group.

- You can raise funds, both in the community and in school, as a school group. The fund raising may have to conform to school policies; for example, we had to use the school's bank account, and though we could run raffles, lotteries (considered to be gambling) were forbidden.

- Other students can also learn from the trip, especially if your colleagues are willing to give some class time to it.

If the school simply refuses to sponsor the trip, *do you want to go on with this project?* Who will pay for adequate liability insurance for you? Where will you meet the students as you prepare to go? Who will pay for your substitute? Will the school even allow you—or the students—to miss class time? Denied sponsorship by the school, I would put the whole idea on the back burner until events (a change in administration, an outpouring of public support for the trip) cleared the way for a change of policy.

When will we go?

The answer to this and other questions will depend on various influences and events. To figure out when is the best time to go, consult the school calendar, your travel agent, and your counterpart, if you have one; here are some questions which may help you.

- When are your school's holidays?

- When are there exams, or periods of intense pressure, for your students?

- Are there special school-wide events that might conflict with the trip? For example, every year the social studies department at my school sponsors a model legislature, in which nearly the whole school takes part.

- Do some dates qualify for "off-season" rates on airlines or at hotels? Airline fares may also vary according to which day of the week you travel, how long you stay, and how far in advance you buy your tickets.

- Does the host country have special holidays that might be especially interesting, or that might complicate travel and sightseeing?

- What dates suit your host community? If you don't have one yet, you should keep the dates tentative until you can take your hosts into account.

In an exchange, you must also figure out when the other group will visit your community. The first Swiss group visited Brattleboro in April; their stay included two weeks when the Americans had school, and one vacation week. I found it hard to teach my classes, host the chaperones, coordinate the students' visit at school (although they often had other sightseeing to do during school hours) and help the families arrange other activities. Besides, April is "mud season" in Vermont, too late for winter sports and too early for pleasant spring weather; October, December, or May would have been more agreeable.

Our second Swiss group came in the summer, because they weren't allowed to miss so much school in Geneva. This plan also had its drawbacks: for one thing, most of the American students had to work during the summer, so the responsibility for the Swiss fell on their families and on those members of the group who weren't working. Also, since the Swiss students were here during the summer when they had no school, and since the program wasn't linked to their school program, a few of the Swiss students seemed to consider their stay as pure vacation. Some of the American families were disappointed that the students seemed more interested in getting together for parties than in being with the families and learning about their everyday lives. On the other hand, there are lots of things to do in Vermont in the summer, so the families (individually and collectively) could offer their visitors a greater variety of activities than at any other season. I personally found the summer visit easier; not having to teach, I could devote myself to the exchange full time.

You and the families will simply have to weigh the advantages and disadvantages of any set of dates for your trip and for receiving your guests, taking the counterparts' preferences into account. A frank discussion of the good and bad points of any calendar will not only make the final decision fairer, but will also help the families to know what to expect when the time comes.

How long will we be gone?

Here, too, your answer will depend on the answers to other questions:

- How long have you been invited to stay with families? If you're planning an exchange, how long do you wish to entertain your guests?

■ How far away are you going? The farther you're traveling, the longer you'll probably want to stay, in order to justify the cost of getting there.

■ How long a stay can your students afford? (See "How much will it cost?" below.) You may want to figure the cost of a shorter trip and a longer one, and let the group choose between them.

■ How much school can the students miss? This may depend on the school's policy or on the students themselves.

How much will it cost?

Money will come up again and again both while you're planning the trip and during the trip itself. Money worries can threaten to dominate the whole experience for you and your students. No matter what you do, some students may worry about whether they have enough money and whether the trip is worth what they're spending, but you can keep their anxiety under control if you anticipate it. First of all, *estimate high* when you plan your budget. Of course you will try to keep the actual cost to a bare minimum, but estimate high to allow for rising prices and unexpected, unavoidable expenses. Prices don't seem to drop, and if you estimate too low and the students have to come up with more money, they will resent it. If the trip ends up costing less than you estimated, the students will be grateful.

Your estimate of the trip's cost must be clearly itemized, so that the students know what's included in the price you quote and what they will have to pay for themselves out of pocket. For example, one trip to Paris might include transportation from home to the airport, trans-Atlantic airfare, and lodging in Paris, including breakfast. The students would need money for everything else, including transportation into the center of Paris, their meals, transportation around the city, and all their entertainment and admissions to museums and monuments. A different arrangement might include a chartered bus to meet them at the airport and to transport them to tourist attractions during their stay; it might provide for all their meals and entertainment. A third plan might combine elements of the two. I chose to include everything I could think of, even though the group took public transportation everywhere and didn't eat meals together; I simply doled out money for those and other expenses at two points during the stay. In this way the students could pay all their expenses ahead of time, but they still had the responsibility of budgeting their money. Some saved enough on food to buy some souvenirs with the extra. Whether you prefer to collect only the money you'll need in advance (e.g., for airline or hotel reservations), or to collect the whole sum and dole it out, will depend on the students' wishes, their maturity, and how much control you want to maintain over them: if you have their dinner money, they'll probably be back for dinner. In any case, the students know how much the trip will cost.

Now let's move from the general to the specific. Your budget may include the following items:

■ Postage to arrange the trip, if the school doesn't pay for it;

■ The cost of any orientation activities you've planned (for example, see "Orientation dinner," Chapter 9);

■ Transportation in the U.S.;

■ International travel;

■ Health insurance (see below);

■ Liability insurance (see below);

- Lodging;

- Meals;

- Transportation within the foreign country;

- Admission to cultural events, tourist attractions, entertainment;

- Payment for any guides or supplementary classes (see "Language/culture lessons," Chapter 4);

- Phone calls to each student during the homestay;

- Communication with school or parents at home;

- The expenses of the leader or leaders, divided among the students (see especially "How will you get around?" Chapter 5);

- A gift from your group to your counterpart;

- A party for the host families at the end of the homestay (see "Help the students show gratitude," Chapter 13);

- A "slush fund" or "emergency fund"—money not budgeted for any specific purpose, but available for unexpected expenses like emergency medical care, a long-distance phone call, even taxi fare for the whole group on a rainy night. Of course, if an individual student draws on the fund, he or she should reimburse it; and of course you'll refund this and any other unspent money, but it can save you a lot of worry and time. I've found that parents understand the importance of this fund and are happy to give the peace of mind it can provide.

Who will get to go?

Once again, the answer to this will depend on your answers to other questions. It's helpful to discuss them with a colleague: conditions vary tremendously from one school to another, and someone else can help you determine fair and realistic requirements for participation, given your school's policies and its students.

- Must the students be in at least a certain grade or class? Must they be at least a certain age?

- Must the students have a certain academic standing? If not, how will you deal with your colleagues' displeasure that a marginal student may miss class?

- Must the students be in a foreign language class (if you're going to a country where a different language is spoken) or demonstrate some degree of competence in a foreign language? Who will judge that competence? How? The foreign trips at my school are sponsored by the foreign language department to supplement the curriculum and to give students a concrete reason to learn languages. We require that students be enrolled in a language class if they take part in these trips.

- Must they help with fund raising? If so, how will you enforce their participation? (see Chapter 8)

- Must they take part in orientation for the trip? If you make participation in orientation a requirement, students will take it seriously. If not, they'll tend to think of the meetings as informative: they say, "I'll be able to get it from someone else." They don't always see that "getting it" secondhand is very different from going through the various processes themselves. Fund-raising and orientation activities build cooperation and trust within the group, which may be formed of people who don't know each other at all. A student who rarely takes part in these activities will not only need a lot of special attention, which will irritate the others; he or she will also feel left out, because the other students, strangers to each other at the beginning, will all be friends.

- Is there any provision (scholarship, special funds) for students who can't afford to pay for the whole trip themselves? This question always comes up when our trips come before the school board for its approval. We always answer, truthfully, that we announce the trips so far ahead of time that almost any student who wants to go can earn the money he or she needs. In fact, as Brattleboro isn't a wealthy community, almost all of the students do earn at least some of the cost of the trip, and many pay for the whole thing themselves.

- Must the students maintain certain standards of behavior at school in order to go? If so, what are they? I would feel very uneasy about taking someone who cut class regularly, or habitually broke school rules. This hasn't been a serious problem so far; the students wait until the trip is over and *then* they stop going to class.

- How many students can you take? Will you select them according to some of the requirements (e.g., we give preference to older and more advanced language students), or will you choose them according to some judgment of their worthiness (based on grades or interviews or recommendations or essays), or will you simply take them on a first-come, first-served basis?

- Do you want to set a deadline for joining the group or for dropping out? It would be too bad to have one student casually drop out when it's already too late for another student to earn the money for the trip or to take part in the group's fund raising and orientation. Besides, as people drop out the trip becomes more expensive for the ones who are left, since they're sharing the leader's expenses. A deadline for paying a non-refundable deposit helps confirm their commitment.

In every way, requirements for participation should encourage students' commitment to the group. Once you've thought out the requirements, they should apply to everyone; if circumstances make you change them, the changes, too, should apply to everyone.

An efficient way to get all the information you need is to make up an application form including whatever questions you'd like the students to answer; it may help you sort out which students are eligible or which ones should go if you have more applicants than places in the group. (See "Have students fill out an application," Chapter 6.)

How will we travel? Where will we stay?

At first general answers are more important than specific ones.

- How will you get to your point of departure?

- Will the international travel be by bus, train or plane? How long will it take?

- Once in the host country, will you charter transportation or use public transportation? What is the public transportation where you'll be going?

- Will you stay in youth hostels or hotels? What will they be like? Will each room have a bathroom? How many students will share a room?

- What's the homestay community like?

When one of our groups decided to go to Paris on the way to Geneva, I made reservations at a small student hotel on the Left Bank where I'd stayed a couple of times. I warned the group that though the hotel was clean, well located, and very inexpensive, it was old and rustic: it had one toilet and one shower per floor, not one of each in every room. When we arrived, we found painters putting the finishing touches on massive renovations: every room had new wallpaper, carpeting, and a brand-new bathroom. "Gee, I thought you said this hotel was old!" said one student—but we were all delighted. The opposite has also happened. Arriving in Montreal one December day, some students, my husband, and I found that our student hotel had been converted to a youth hostel: there were two or more bunkbeds in each room and no sheets, blankets or towels to be had. The students managed to rise gracefully to the occasion, but they did say they wished they'd *known*.

Why will we meet before the trip? How often?

Before you decide on the answer to these questions, you might want to read the chapters on fund raising and, particularly, orientation: both of these activities demand a great deal of commitment from the group—a commitment that is repaid over and over again during the travel, when the students know each other and know that they are prepared.

In addition to the regular group meetings, students can meet naturally and easily if they are all in one class—or one homeroom, if that can be arranged in your school. That way you can answer individual questions as they come up. As the students' homeroom teacher, you can also get to know them easily: you naturally become aware of their attendance patterns and their general attitude toward school and other students. On the whole, the better you know your students, the easier the trip will be for you.

If your group is dispersed among several classes, leave plenty of opportunity during group meetings for students to ask their individual questions. Even if you do this, they may want to take advantage of seeing you in class to talk about the trip. When there are some students in a class who won't be going, insist that the participants save their questions until after class; the students who aren't going will be grateful.

Choose your co-leader

If your group numbers 10 or fewer students, you may take complete charge of it yourself; a larger group requires more supervision than one person can provide. My school board now requires two adults on student trips abroad, no matter how small the group. They made that decision after one of the leaders of a group from a nearby school dropped dead of a heart attack in Paris. Fortunately a second leader was there to deal with the situation, but even if nothing goes seriously wrong a co-leader can be a great help: one leader can go to the bank while the other deals with the hotel; if a few of the students are late, one of the leaders can wait for them while the other goes on ahead with the others; if a student is sick, one leader can stay with that student or take him or her to a doctor; and so on.

You may not have the luxury of choosing your co-leader. If you do, think carefully before inviting anyone to help. A number of parents and teachers may express an interest in going. Some people think of the trip as a vacation with all expenses paid, so before you commit yourself to anyone, ask yourself the following questions:

■ Does this person like and understand students of this age? If the answer is no, go no further: this person could ruin the trip for everyone.

- Do the students know the person? They don't need to know him or her, but it helps if they do.

- Will the students like and respect the person? If they don't know him or her, it's hard to predict how they'll react, but liking and respect on both sides are essential.

- Will this person willingly take responsibility before, during, and after the trip? He or she must take responsibility not only for the students during the trip itself, but also for fund raising, for making arrangements, for orientation, for follow-up—for all that goes into making the trip more than a simple tour. The two of you can divide up the tasks and responsibilities any way that suits you, but you should share them fairly.

     Be sure that the co-leader understands that you both will remain with the group throughout the trip. Of course each leader will need a few hours away from the group now and then, and you should arrange the schedule to allow that time. Still, the leaders' first obligation is to the students.

- Will this person take the time to participate in all the meetings, orientation, and other preparations? Even if you've agreed that organizing these activities is your responsibility, the other person must take part: he or she will develop a comfortable working relationship with the students, and the parents will have a chance to get to know and trust him or her.

- Does this person have a positive attitude? There will be plenty of problems, large and small; you need someone who can deal with them comfortably, learn from them, and when all else fails, laugh about them.

I believe that these questions are more important than whether the person speaks the language well or has already traveled in the country, although those may be important considerations if you are a completely inexperienced traveler yourself. The trip's purpose is to help the students learn, and you should look for someone who understands that goal and can complement your skills while sharing the responsibility involved.

What are the rules?

Students probably won't ask this question, nor will they ask, "Can we drink?" "Will we have to do what the group does, or can we go off on our own—or stay in the hotel?" "What's the story on drugs?" "What happens if we get caught breaking the rules?" Still, you should give serious consideration to what rules you'll need, why, and how you'll enforce them. After all, in the eyes of the community, the law (at least to some extent), the school, and finally, the students' parents, you are responsible for those students. You're responsible for their well-being and for their behavior. It's up to you to lay out clear guidelines, so that you can feel comfortable with your responsibility and they can feel comfortable with you.

     First you should talk with the principal to find out whether the school has policies that govern the behavior of students on trips. If you think some of those policies would be impossible to enforce, or inappropriate in another culture, or if you have any reservations about them, you should discuss your reservations openly with the principal; otherwise he or she will assume that you are following the usual guidelines.

     When you're explaining the rules to the group, *don't assume anything*. Naturally, students would prefer to be on their own, and they won't have thought about limitations on their behavior, so don't wait for something to go wrong before you bring up the subject.

Explain that you are responsible for them, and then explain—in detail, and in practical terms—the reason for each rule. Most students are willing to think about these questions and to look at them from your point of view. If they trust you, they'll take your word on things they might not know about, such as what is or isn't acceptable behavior in the host country.

During the preparation and the trip itself, don't hesitate to remind the students what the rules are and why they're necessary. If you change a rule, even to relax it, you owe it to the students to explain the change as thoroughly as you discussed your original reasoning; otherwise they figure that you didn't take that rule (or, by extension, any of the others) seriously in the first place—so why should they?

Now to specifics:

ALCOHOL. To American teenagers, drinking often represents freedom, glamor, and being an adult. Some are very cool about it: on one trip to Montreal with a group of students from a private school, I was astonished to find a few of them drinking Bloody Marys in the club car of our train—at 7:00 in the morning. "Oh, don't worry, Maggie," one 14-year-old girl said, trying to reassure me, "I can hold my liquor." At the same time, temptation is everywhere during a student trip, because many cultures are much more relaxed about alcohol than Americans are. Unless you're with the students every minute of every day, you can't actually prevent them from drinking.

Alcohol can cause serious problems on a trip; for one thing, the 14-year-old notwithstanding, teenagers often don't know their capacity and end up drinking far more than they can handle—and drunken adolescents are, paradoxically, less acceptable in other cultures than in ours; drunken American students are especially conspicuous. Even if students don't go to such extremes, if they drink without any restrictions and then come home and brag about it, you may get into trouble with school authorities or with the students' parents.

Dan and I had set a very strict no-alcohol policy for our group's two-day stay in Paris. We reasoned that the students would be suffering from jet lag, so they wouldn't physically be able to handle alcohol; besides, we had so little time in Paris that we didn't want them to spend it in bars, and we wanted them to be in top form to meet their Swiss homestay families. The students seemed to go along with the rule until the final evening. A former student from our high school, who was living and working in Paris, invited the whole group—27 of us—to her apartment for a party. She told me that she and her friends were planning to serve some wine, and I didn't object, figuring that we would be there to keep an eye on things. Relaxing the no-alcohol rule was our first mistake. We told the students that they were still more tired than they realized, and that they should take it very easy. At the party, a young man continually filled and refilled the glass of one of our students, whom I'll call Pete. We didn't know what had happened until after the party, when we saw Pete weaving down the sidewalk. The Métro was his undoing: he threw up all over himself, the subway car, and the stunned Parisian nearby. He threw up at the hotel, and the next morning he threw up in the railroad station. In the train to Geneva, he asked in a weak voice, "How can I tell my homestay family in French that I don't want to drink at all?" From time to time, as the train sped down through France, I could hear him repeating under his breath, "Non, merci. Je ne bois pas de boissons alcoolisées."

He was learning his lesson; Dan and I still had a lot to learn. Feeling that we'd been responsible for the presence of the wine at the party, and seeing how much Pete was suffering, we didn't punish him further. We should have met with the whole group and discussed the situation openly with them. We didn't, so a couple of students assumed we wouldn't punish them for drinking, either. As we found out only much later (too late to do anything), drinking became the focus of their two-week stay in Geneva.

After all this, I wish I knew some simple answers to the question of drinking. Unless your students are exceptionally self-disciplined, merely forbidding it will only guarantee that they will try to hide any drinking they do. I think clear guidelines (even, *"One* glass of wine with dinner," if that's appropriate), explanations for the guidelines, and—most of all —keeping in touch with individual students will help you spot trouble and head it off. Talk with the individual students, show them that you're concerned. If necessary, keep a closer eye on them until you're sure that they've got the message and will take more responsibility for themselves. They should understand that you're keeping in touch with them not to punish them but to keep things running smoothly for everybody.

DRUGS. Just as many other cultures accept moderate alcohol use by teenagers, many segments of American culture accept, at least tacitly, moderate drug use. Some other countries are much stricter about it.

We make it a point to tell the students during the group's first meetings that if they get into legal trouble with drugs, we refuse to take further responsibility for them; we'll notify their parents and the school, and then they're on their own. We tell their parents and the principal the same thing. So far, we've been lucky enough not to have this problem on any long trips.

Of course, not all students who use drugs get into trouble with the law. If you think someone might be using drugs, it won't hurt to talk privately with that student as you would with someone who might be misusing alcohol; you might be able to nip trouble in the bud.

STEALING. It never occurred to me to discuss stealing with the group or to have a rule against it, but Dan and I discovered on a recent trip that some students were systematically taking "souvenirs"—ashtrays or marked glasses—from restaurants, cafés, and even a big wine-making cooperative where we'd been guests for a tour and a wine tasting. When we confronted the students we thought were involved (there may have been others, too), their reactions ranged from extreme embarrassment to irritation. Once again, if we'd foreseen the problem and talked about it beforehand, we would have headed it off, at least for most of the students. They probably didn't think about it at all in advance, but if we'd explained that taking such "souvenirs" violates hospitality, is in fact stealing, and reflects badly on the group as a whole, they probably would have held back.

SEX. Everyone would probably prefer not to talk about sexual conduct, but you may want to bring it up anyway: questions may arise during the trip, especially if the group is going to spend most of its time in hotels or if there are obvious couples within the group. It's a touchy subject because it's so personal, and it doesn't lend itself to rules. If you are considering making rules (e.g., forbidding girls to go into boys' rooms and vice versa), you should know how you intend to enforce them. Are you going to patrol the corridor? What will you do if you find girls and boys gathered in someone's room to watch TV?

If you prefer to rely on the students' good judgment, you—and they—should know what you mean by good judgment. One way of handling the question is to tell them that they'd better not get involved in anything they wouldn't want everyone (including the people back home) to know about: privacy is almost nonexistent and gossip is inevitable when the group spends so much time together and everyone is so dependent on everyone else. Then if someone's behavior is getting out of line, you can talk privately with that student (or the couple, if both are in the group) before things get out of hand. If you act quickly, there will be time for the behavior to improve before you have to take any drastic action.

STAYING WITH THE GROUP. You may wish to require your students to stay with the group at times; at other times it may be OK for them to explore on their own, or in twos and threes. These decisions may depend on how big a town or city is, how safe it seems, how mature your students are, and what you've agreed on with the parents or the school (for example, it reassures all parties to know that the group will be with the leaders after dark in big cities). You needn't account for every second of the trip in advance; it's enough to let the parents and students know that when the time comes you'll expect to decide when they may be on their own.

You might want to say in so many words that when they aren't with the whole group, students are not to go off with people they've just met. International friendships can spring up in hours, like mushrooms: on one weekend trip to Montreal, one of our students met a Canadian boy on Saturday afternoon. When we got up Sunday morning, she'd already left the hotel to meet his family. She returned too late to leave on the train with the others, so she and I shared a long, uncomfortable, and mostly silent bus-ride back to school. (See "Losing someone," Chapter 12.)

Sometimes students don't know how to say no gracefully on their own, and it helps them to know they can use you as an excuse. On a later trip to Montreal, two of our students met two young Canadian men at the disco in our hotel. After animated conversation, the young men (lumberjacks on leave from the northern woods of Quebec) invited the girls to a friend's apartment. "But we told them our teacher would kill us if we left the disco," one of the girls said the next day. Everybody saved face, and the girls stayed where they belonged.

If your students meet people they'd like to spend more time with, you can encourage them to invite their new friends to spend some time with the group. All the students may learn a lot from them, and at the same time you can get to know them in an informal way.

FREE TIME. How you expect your students to spend their free time while they're abroad will depend on how much they have. If you're planning to allow them a lot of time on their own, but you expect them to use it doing or seeing certain things, the time isn't really free, and they should know that right from the start. Free time is time to do what *they* want to do. You can limit how much they have, and you can certainly expect that they *won't* do certain things (e.g., drink, or leave a certain area), but beyond that, there's no reason to control their use of that time.

As you talk with the students about what they've done with their unstructured time, if you find that some don't seem to be using it constructively, it's better to zero in on those individuals than to regiment the entire group. It's too bad to restrict all the students (most of whom will learn a lot on their own) in order to keep tabs on a few. Depending on the situation, you can suggest things for them to do, require that they do these things, offer to go with them, invite them to go with you, or *require* them to go with you. Explaining your expectations and the possible consequences if students don't live up to them will encourage everyone to use their free time well.

Sending a student home

Situations, policies, and personalities vary so much that there's no way to foresee the exact combination that would make you send a student home. Everyone involved in the trip—especially you—will hope that you never even have to think about it, and you probably won't have to. Still, you should make it clear from the outset that you will send students home, at their own expense, if you think they're causing serious problems for themselves, other students, their host families, or you. I emphasize that if a student has to return early, for whatever reason, the expense can run into hundreds of dollars: if the group has a special round-trip fare, often a change in plans means that the student must forfeit the difference between the special fare and the regular fare *both ways.*

Before the problem gets that serious, try to get in touch with the student's parents. They deserve to know what's going on, and they may be able to have some influence. A collect call will be expensive, but it's a lot cheaper than return airfare would be. At the same time, you might want to let someone at school know what's happening, in order to get another perspective on the problem and to share the responsibility.

Actually sending a student home will clearly be a last resort: you must be convinced that he or she is either unable or unwilling to change the behavior that's causing the problem. Once you've reached this conclusion, and have consulted the parents and the school, there's no reason to delay: put the student on a plane as soon as you can, and turn your attention back to the rest of the group.

Rules are unpleasant because they bring with them thoughts of all the things that could go wrong. There's no need to dwell on them, but think of them and present them to the group as indications of what behavior you and the school expect of them.

Insurance

You should consider at least two kinds of coverage: liability insurance for yourself, and a uniform health insurance policy for yourself and the students.

As I've mentioned, when you set off with a group of students, you take on responsibility for them. If one of the students accidentally pushes someone through a bank's plate-glass window, the victim—or the bank, or both—may want to blame the nearest responsible adult: you. If something happens to a student, his or her family may want to sue. Liability insurance protects you. Your school may already have a substantial policy for its teachers (see "Is this a school-sponsored trip?" earlier in this chapter). If so, check with the school's insurance agent to be sure the policy covers you if you're out of the country, and if a case is brought in a foreign court. The policy may need a special rider to cover your particular situation; if so, ask the school to pay for it. If the school has no liability insurance coverage for its teachers, you may still want to get some for yourself. Ask an insurance agent for information; also check with your teachers' association or union, as many professional organizations offer low-cost group coverage. If the school does not pay for this insurance, the group should.

Most of your students will probably already have some health insurance, but I've required students to purchase a uniform health and accident policy. I tell the families frankly that I don't want to deal with 25 different forms and companies. They've readily accepted the idea, especially since the school's insurance agent was able to find an inexpensive policy. It took some research, because the premiums for such a short-term policy are so low that some companies don't want to be bothered with it.

So far I haven't actually had to use the policies, but that's just luck: an American girl in another Swiss exchange fell while skiing near Zermatt and required a helicopter to take her to a hospital in Geneva. So you never know.

Get all this on paper: preliminary information sheet, Conditions of Participation

If you write down the particulars of your trip, you can distribute the information to school authorities, to interested students, and to their parents, and you won't have to repeat yourself a hundred times and wonder if you've left something out. You can write the information as a narrative ("We'll spend three days in Köln, sightseeing. If possible we'll stay in a youth hostel") or as questions and answers, or as an outline. Whatever the format, keep the language clear and informal, so you won't overwhelm your reader.

At first all you'll need is preliminary information: dates, main activities, cost, who's eligible and what you expect from participants. You probably won't have details like which airline you'll take, exactly where you will stay or exactly what you'll do. Later, when you have all that information, you can write it out for whoever needs it: students, parents, your counterpart, school administrators, maybe the local press.

Here on the next two pages are samples of the first items we hand out to prospective travelers; then, if they and their parents are still interested, we give them an application (see "Have students fill out applications," Chapter 6).

Get formal approval from school authorities

Now you're ready to go to the principal, headmaster, headmistress, superintendent, or school committee to get formal approval for the trip. Tell them why you think the trip is important, and then present the information you've written up. You may also want to include a word about your own travel experience.

If the trip wins official approval, it might be a good idea to get the approval in writing; if the approval is in the form of a motion at a school committee meeting, the minutes will serve as a public written record of the committee's action. The more complete your written presentation, the more comprehensive the school's backing can be. If the school is paying for anything associated with the trip, that financial commitment should be especially clear.

So, if all goes well, the trip has now gone from a vague idea to an official, school-sponsored activity. Now to assemble your group of travelers!

Preliminary Information Sheet

Echange avec la Suisse

Dates

Swiss here: last two weeks in October of next year (Saturday to Saturday; the weekend between the two weeks is a four-day holiday for BUHS students).

Americans in Switzerland: the homestay in Geneva will take place April vacation and the week before it; if the group goes to Paris first (that decision will rest with the group, after it has considered the extra expense), it will leave 1½ weeks before April vacation.

Requirements

■ a commitment to the homestay as the heart of the program, both for the Americans and for their Swiss partners. BUHS students who work *must* make arrangements with their employers so that they will have time to spend with their counterparts.

■ a commitment to using French while in France and Switzerland.

■ enrollment in a French class (level 2–5).

■ participants must be juniors or seniors in 1988–89.

■ participants must be able to attend *all* orientation sessions and meetings to plan the Swiss visit.

■ students and their parents must read and sign the Conditions of Participation form.

Cost

The final price of the exchange will depend on the exchange rate of the dollar in France and Switzerland. We will work with a travel-agent to get the lowest reasonable air-fares, etc. We *estimate* the price per student to be:

Swiss visit: $175.00. BUHS participants are responsible for planning and paying for activities to help the Swiss understand and enjoy their homestay in Vermont.

Two-day stay in Paris, transportation Brattleboro-Paris-Geneva-Brattleboro: $1000–$1200, depending on the exchange rate. The Swiss will organize and pay for group activities in Geneva.

The price per student includes a share of the chaperones' expenses.

Individual students can save a great deal of money by working on group fundraising.

Orientation

Orientation will take place after school. We will try to schedule those meetings so that all interested students can attend; at the same time, orientation is an essential part of the exchange and students must take part in orientation in order to go to Europe.

Leaders

Ms. Libby and Ms. Cassidy will work together to help students plan the Swiss students' stay, to prepare the BUHS students for their trip, and to accompany the group to Europe.

Please note: Until the BUHS Board approves this exchange, our organizational efforts are preliminary and unofficial. The Board has enthusiastically supported all four previous exchanges.

BUHS ABROAD

Conditions of Participation

1. Participants must be juniors or seniors enrolled in French 2–5.

2. Each student must take a great deal of responsibility during the entire exchange. Responsibilities include:

- regular attendance at school (right up to the day of departure, and after the group's return);
- active participation in orientation sessions;
- working with the leaders and other participants to prepare and organize the Swiss students' homestay in Brattleboro. BUHS students who work must make arrangements with their employers so they will have time to spend with their counterparts;
- commitment to speaking French during the trip;
- working with the group during the stay in France and the Swiss family during the homestay in Geneva to make those experiences pleasant and educational for all involved.

3. Students will earn 1 academic credit (on their transcripts but not fulfilling graduation requirements) for successfully completing orientation sessions, a journal, a project, and a final evaluation.

4. Participants will not always be under the direct supervision of leaders; in pairs and small groups, they will find their own way around Paris during the day. However, during the stay in France *no* student is to go alone anywhere outside the hotel after dark; adult leaders will accompany all group activities in the evening.

5. The price of the program will be based on the number of participants. If a student drops out or is asked to leave the program *for any reason,* BUHS Abroad will refund whatever part of the student's deposit it can *without raising the cost to other participants.*

All money raised by the group is the property of the group, and no portion may be withdrawn by a student who drops out of the exchange. A work-bank system will distribute the total raised in proportion to the time and effort contributed by each student. The group's money may be used only to defray the cost of the program.

6. BUHS Abroad leaders may send any student home for:

- behavior that endangers the student's or anyone else's health and welfare, e.g. alcohol or drug abuse;
- behavior that seriously disturbs the homestay family or the group;
- failing to obey local laws or standards of behavior;
- insubordination.

STUDENTS SENT HOME UNDER THESE CONDITIONS MUST PAY ANY EXTRA EXPENSES ASSOCIATED WITH THEIR PREMATURE RETURN.

3

Talk with Students and Their Parents

The next step is to get your group together. I've put meeting with the students and their parents in the same chapter because usually teenagers can't undertake a project this big unless they have at least tacit support from their families. You'll find that if that support is explicit, you can draw on it as the trip develops: you and the students and their parents can all work together and all will benefit. Communication will be easier if you establish it at the outset.

Find Interested Students

Now that the school is sponsoring your trip, you can use the school to find suitable students.

Talk with appropriate classes

Of course, you'll want to talk with any of your own classes that have qualified students in them. Also ask your colleagues if you can come into their classes to talk with students who might be eligible for the trip and interested in it. These might include classes in geography, history, foreign language, English, vocational subjects, music, or art, depending on the trip's destination and purpose.

At this time there's no need to go into much detail. You can simply hand out a preliminary information sheet and/or the Conditions of Membership, answer a few general questions about the trip, and tell interested students that you will schedule a meeting to give them more detailed information. If you've already scheduled the meeting and can tell them right away when and where it will be, so much the better.

You may wish to hand out applications at this time. Please see "Have students fill out applications" in Chapter 6.

Publicize an informational meeting

It's to your advantage to get as many students as possible to your informational session: interested students who miss it will ask for the information one by one in the days to come (often at strikingly inconvenient times, when you're rushing to a meeting or to answer a long-distance phone call). So publicize the meeting beforehand: ask someone on the school newspaper to write a short article including the details of the meeting; put announcements on the public address system; put up posters in strategic places around school; remind your own students of it and ask them to remind their friends.

Meet with interested students

This first meeting can set the tone for the whole trip. Hand out the information sheets you prepared, and go through them point by point with the students. They may need settling down or reassurance: settling down as they think about being far away from their parents and the school, reassurance as they wonder about raising enough money or really speaking a foreign language or living with a family. As they need settling down, go over the rules with them, explaining how you arrived at them and why they are necessary. When they need reassurance, point out that they have plenty of time to earn money, and that the group can work together to raise some; remind them that they also have lots of time to prepare for other aspects of the trip—and that you've planned orientation activities to help them do just that.

Before they leave the meeting, be sure you've found out from them what free time they have during a typical week, so you can schedule regular orientation sessions. Also find out when their parents are free to attend an informational meeting; this will probably have to be in the evening to accommodate working families.

It's possible to combine the first meetings for parents and for students into one. I prefer to meet with students first, to get an idea of which students are interested and to answer their questions, which they may be shy about asking at a first meeting that includes parents.

Meet with the Parents—and Their Children

Invite school administrators
if it's appropriate

Particularly if this is the first trip you've taken with students from your school, you may want to invite one or more administrators to the meeting with parents; they can answer policy questions on the spot, and their presence shows that the school is supporting the trip. I asked the head of my department to attend that first meeting with the parents. He answered some of the parents' questions there, and then later, as the group prepared for the trip, he knew the people involved well enough to take them into account as he gave me suggestions.

Present the basic information

As with the students, the easiest way to cover all the material with their parents is to hand out information sheets and talk over each section. It won't hurt the students to hear the essential information again, and it's good for them to hear the parents' questions, which will probably differ from the ones the students themselves asked. It's even helpful to ask the parents to go over the requirements for participation again with their children at home; this reinforcement will let the students know that they can't play you and their parents off against each other.

Define your role

It's important to define clearly the limits of your responsibility. Before they allow their children to take part in the trip, the parents should know how much you intend to supervise the students during the trip and how you expect them to use their unsupervised time. When the parents first realize that you won't—can't possibly—be looking over their children's shoulders 24 hours a day, they will feel understandably nervous about sending them so far away. Letting them know how often you *will* meet with the students will allay the parents' nervousness.

You may also wish to talk with the parents about your responsibility—and theirs— before and after the trip as well as during it. For example, do you want to supervise the fund raising, or do you expect the parents to be responsible for it? Do you want them to keep track of the money the group raises, or does your school require that you do that, as school advisor to the group? If you're involved in an exchange, do you want the parents to help you organize your guests' stay? Or do you want to help them?

It's not too soon to discuss how to carry out these responsibilities. The parents and students can decide to act as a whole group, or they can elect or appoint a steering committee, with the understanding that the committee will call on everyone as the need arises. Or they can appoint various committees for various tasks as they go along.

Depending on when you hand out applications, when they must be returned, and when you get permission from the school board, the group may still be taking shape at this point; in that case you need to meet again—students, parents, and leaders—in a few weeks so the actual participants can make a final decision on how the group will proceed.

Money—again

Money may concern the parents even more than it does the students. They will be especially concerned about hidden costs, but if your itemized budget is clear they'll be able to see what they'll be paying for.

Parents and students may wonder why the group should pay your expenses. I don't wait for them to ask about it, as such a question might be embarrassing for everyone. When we reach that item in the budget, I explain that what might seem a free vacation at first glance is just the opposite: a leader not only takes on 24-hour-a-day responsibility while the group is abroad, but also must put in innumerable hours to plan the trip, plan and carry out orientation activities, and help with fund raising. None of that work is paid, nor need it be, but when the leader's expenses are divided among all the students in the group, they're getting a lot for their money.

Both students and parents will want to know how much money the group can raise. As with other aspects of the money question, it's best not to raise everyone's expectations too high. I generally encourage students to plan on paying the whole amount budgeted; then whatever they earn as a group will lessen that amount. If you and the students have a great deal of experience raising money, you may feel confident in naming an amount that will be your fund-raising goal. Chapter 8 will give you some ideas for ways to earn money.

At the same time, you may want to discuss how to distribute whatever money the group does raise. Some groups develop systems to keep track of the amount of time or effort each person puts into the group's fund-raising efforts, and then distribute the money earned in proportion to each person's contribution (see "The work bank" in Chapter 8). Good fund-raising activities can be more lucrative for participants than even a great job, and this system provides an incentive to students to work with the group.

Whether or not you use a work bank, probably all the proceeds from group fund-raising efforts should belong to the group, and individuals who drop out should not expect to get any cash back from their efforts, no matter how much time they put into fund raising. As with other aspects of the trip, it's important to state this from the beginning to avoid any misunderstandings or hard feelings later on.

Preliminary permission form

You can get at least a rough idea of which students are seriously interested if you require them and their parents to sign a preliminary permission form. Make it open-ended, so that they're not absolutely committed to going and you're not absolutely committed to taking them. It indicates their interest, their commitment to orientation and fund-raising activities, and their agreement to whatever decision you or the group made about how to distribute the group's funds.

The speed with which the students return the slip indicates fairly accurately the enthusiasm of both the students and their parents. You may even want to give preference to those who bring back the signed forms first, though enthusiasm isn't always the best single qualification for a trip.

Of course, if you have already distributed applications, the signed application can take the place of a preliminary permission form.

4

Plan the Details of the Trip

The planning you must do depends on whether you have a counterpart in your host community and how much that person is willing to do for you in the way of suggesting interesting activities, making reservations, and arranging tours for your group. Without a homestay, of course, you're on your own to do all the planning. If you're organizing an exchange, you and your counterpart may find it best to leave the planning for each side of the exchange to the hosts. Obviously it's more convenient for the people on the spot to arrange the details of a visit, but letting the hosts plan the visits has another important result. In this arrangement the families on each side don't merely provide a place to stay—they're *hosts;* the visitors aren't just tourists—they're *guests.* The relationship between hosts and guests can be more complex and at the same time much more rewarding than the relationship between foreign visitors and providers-of-room-and-board. For example, the hosts may want to show their guests a local business or historical site as well as standard tourist attractions in their area. At times the guests may not even understand exactly why they're going to see something that may seem trivial or boring; on the other hand, if they get involved, ask questions, and finally succeed in understanding its importance to their hosts, they'll have learned more about the new country than they could have learned in any other way.

Even if your hosts are planning most of your stay, you should think about what the group will be doing each day. For the most part, you'll probably want to fall in with what your hosts propose, though you should let them know if they seem to be planning too full a schedule, or if your group has particular interests, so they can plan accordingly. For example, in our first exchange with Switzerland, many of our students wanted to see Mont

Blanc; M. Troesch graciously arranged an all-day excursion to Chamonix among the whirl of factory tours, receptions, and wine tastings he'd already planned.

Between the extremes of no homestay at all and hosts who arrange your visit in detail, there's a lot of middle ground. If your counterpart doesn't plan a program for the group during its homestay, you must do so. Or if you have a city-stay in addition to your homestay, you'll have to plan that.

Getting started

You'll need the following information in order to plan a city-stay:

- a map of the city or area you'll be visiting;

- a list of hotels, with their prices;

- information on what public transportation is available, its efficiency and cost;

- a listing, as varied as possible, of museums, monuments, and tourist attractions;

- a list of discos, student clubs, or other places where young people can meet or spend time.

Look for one or more guidebooks that deal with the area you'll be visiting. Your travel agent, librarian, or bookseller may be able to suggest specific titles of some guidebooks. If not, look for a mixture of standard books and offbeat ones aimed at students.

Find a hotel

Before you look for a specific hotel, you may want to consider in what area you want to stay. If you're planning to visit a big city, are there any nearby small towns or suburbs where you might want to look for a place to spend the night? Often hotels are less expensive there than in the central districts, even with the added cost of transportation. If you're assured of inexpensive hotels and convenient, inexpensive transportation into the center of the city, staying outside the city makes sense because the students can take advantage of the city's attractions without being exposed to its dangers or its temptations—unless you're supervising them.

A hotel can be more than a warm bed, a hot shower, and a roof over your head. It can represent the culture you're visiting, and can establish a pleasant ambiance for your stay. For these reasons, I prefer small, family-run hotels to big international hotels. Most countries' standards are reliable enough to ensure that the hotels with a given rating will be clean and comfortable; beyond that, it's the very individuality of the hotel (the stained-glass windows on the stairwell, the woodwork in the lobby, the rolls at breakfast) that the students will remember. Small hotels also encourage students to behave responsibly: the staff may lock the hotel at a given hour, or require the students to be quiet at night in order to let other guests sleep. Big hotels tend to be much more impersonal.

To get the names of specific hotels, consult the guidebooks or your travel agent. It's a good idea to write to a hotel (or a couple, if you want a choice) before actually making reservations. You can ask about group prices, whether breakfast is included (or a package price if breakfast can be included), how far away public transportation is, and any other questions you may have.

Many hotels, whatever their size, hesitate to accept students because they're often so noisy and can cause so much damage to the rooms and furnishings. If your letter includes assurances that the students will be responsible for their behavior, it may help in getting reservations. Make sure the students realize what responsible behavior is (see "Stealing," Chapter 2; if necessary, plan to check rooms as the students leave the hotel): for at least some of them, this will be the first time they've stayed in a hotel without their parents, and without guidance they may abuse their freedom.

Depending on where you're going, a youth hostel may suit your needs. Youth hostels are certainly the least expensive places for young people to stay, and they provide a natural way for your students to meet others from around the world. Some hostels have strict curfews and rules (e.g., no one is to be in the rooms during the day); some, especially the ones located at schools or universities, are open only in the summer; some require visitors to have hostel cards, while others are open to all travelers. As these conditions vary so much from location to location, it's best to get information on the specific hostel in the area you'll be visiting. You may find some information in guidebooks for students; you can get information on hostels that are in the International Youth Hostel Federation by writing to:

American Youth Hostels
Delaplane, Virginia 22025

Eating

There is no need to plan every meal from the time you leave home until the time you return, but thinking about the question in advance will help you provide alternatives to McDonald's, Wendy's, and Wimpy, which seem to attract American students as magnets attract iron filings.

Arranging breakfast at the hotel (and paying for it in advance) encourages the students to eat breakfast, and they'll be healthier and in better spirits if they do. It also gives you a convenient place and time to see individual students. "Please be sure to check with me at breakfast" sounds both more concrete and more agreeable than "Please be sure to check with me before you leave the hotel tomorrow." If the hotel doesn't have facilities for breakfast, or if it doesn't suit you for some reason, search out a nearby café or restaurant that does, and establish that as the breakfast place. Even if students decide not to eat breakfast themselves, or eat it elsewhere, they'll know where to find you at a certain time; besides, encouraging them to eat some breakfast will seem more natural in that setting.

As for other meals, aim for variety. Where, when, and how you eat will naturally depend on where you are and what you're doing on a given day. Sometimes you may want to include picnics, as they're more economical than restaurant meals. They're especially appropriate during a day-long visit to a tourist spot with only a few high-priced restaurants nearby. For further variety, some of the picnics can be in small groups and some can be for the whole group together: collecting the money (in local currency), figuring out appropriate quantities of food and actually buying the provisions can be excellent experiences for your students, so delegate each chore to a team of two or three. In order for these picnics to be fun and a good learning experience, you should allow plenty of time for the teams to do their work, and be ready to guide anyone who needs help and encouragement.

Often the easiest and most appropriate way to get food is simply to split into small groups and eat at various restaurants in a particular area. Now and then during an extended trip, you might want to ask different groups if you can eat with them; they'll probably be pleased, and eating with them gives you the chance to find out how they're doing; furthermore, when you're there to answer their questions about the menu, they may be a little more adventurous about ordering unfamiliar dishes than when they're on their own.

If the group's city-stay lasts more than three or four days, it might be nice to plan one big, relatively formal meal for the whole group at a good restaurant. The meal itself can be an occasion for the students, especially if it comes toward the end of their stay. Like hotels, many restaurants are reluctant to take groups because they can disturb other guests. Visiting the restaurant yourself can help smooth the way for your group: the owner will appreciate your foresight and at the same time you can get an idea of the restaurant's layout, menu, atmosphere, and prices. You may even be able to arrange to have all your students pay a fixed price for a limited menu; this system can work well if there's enough choice available at the price you and your restaurateur agree on. Once again, preparing the students for what they'll experience will give them confidence and make the experience pleasant for them, the restaurant's staff, and you.

Activities

Now that you've figured out where you'll probably be staying and how the group will keep from starving, you should start working toward a day-by-day program for the trip. The further in advance you can come up with at least a tentative plan, the more specific your orientation can be, and the more the students will benefit from the various activities.

Do you want to organize meetings or classes?

Whether you're planning a city-stay or a homestay, you might want to set up regular meetings or classes for the whole group. At the very least, meetings of the whole group provide an opportunity for efficient communication within the group: you and the students can make announcements, squelch rumors, discuss what you'll be doing in the next day or so, and make any necessary collective decisions. The meetings are essential for communication and also remind the students that they're part of a group and can rely on each other, especially if the students spend most of their time alone or in small groups.

You may want to go one step further and set up actual classes, though they would be very different from the classes the students normally have at school. The classes could include any of the following:

STUDY TIME. Particularly if your school administrators or colleagues expect the students to keep up with their classes at home, you can help by organizing some study hours at various points during the trip. Students in homestays may have enough time to do their schoolwork when their counterparts do theirs, but if you're touring, probably very few of your students will take time for their studies unless you build that time into the schedule.

INTRODUCTIONS TO THE NEXT ACTIVITY. You, a host national, or a student can explain the history of a cathedral, the rules of soccer, or what to look for at the ballet. These meetings can be especially useful during homestays; the students might otherwise rush from one activity to another, with little opportunity to think about what's ahead or to talk over their experiences in a meaningful way.

SHARING AND COMPARING. You can discuss what students like about what they're seeing and experiencing, and what makes them uncomfortable. Talking things over can help the students go beyond reacting—either positively or negatively—to their experiences and surroundings; it can help them understand what they're going through and come to terms with it. Talking things over together can also ease the tensions that arise at times during homestays; as long as the students are careful to be discreet about what they say about the host families, they can share their good and bad moments and learn from what everyone else is going through. They can also share other discoveries, like an interesting exhibit or a good place to buy souvenirs.

LANGUAGE/CULTURE LESSONS. A foreign trip is an ideal setting for language learning: the new language is everywhere, and learning to speak and understand it makes the trip immeasurably richer for the students. Lessons can grow naturally out of the group's activities and experiences, whether the students are living with families or not. As most of the students will be struggling simply to understand and speak the language, it's better to put most of the emphasis on those skills rather than on reading and writing, though reading can vary the pace and reinforce their speaking and comprehension: for example, learning to read a local newspaper (first the ads and TV listings, then the articles) can help them understand the place they're visiting.

If you don't feel up to teaching the language lessons yourself, you may be able to arrange for a native speaker in the host country to teach them. You'll almost certainly have to pay the teacher, though in an exchange perhaps you could arrange English lessons for the visitors in return for their finding a language teacher for your group. Ask your counterpart for suggestions, but in any case, be sure to say specifically what sort of lessons you have in mind. Otherwise you might find that the teacher is prepared to teach only the finer points of grammar when your students want to learn how to meet other young people, and what to say when they do. This situation would be unfair to both teacher and class.

For more ideas about language and culture, see Chapter 9; if you don't have time to go through all of the orientation exercises, you can adapt many of them for use when you're already in the country.

Vary the pace of the activities

Traveling is demanding and tiring, and varying the activities you plan will help you minimize your students' fatigue. Look for some activities that call for physical exertion, and others that engage the students' minds or their senses. Plan some all-day outings, some half-day ones; divide the students into small groups for some of the activities, and keep them together for others.

Here are some suggestions for activities that may interest the students:

ARCHITECTURE. Look not only for historical buildings (though old buildings, from castles to cathedrals, have a special fascination for American students because there are so few old buildings in the U.S.), but also for striking examples of modern architecture. Students often have interesting questions and observations about the relationship between architecture and the rest of the culture.

SPORTS. Students might enjoy not only spectator sports like soccer or bullfights or bicycle racing, but also participatory sports: skating, skiing, biking, swimming, volleyball. You can often rent equipment for these activities; ask about group rates and student discounts.

PUBLIC PARKS AND GARDENS. Students might not think of going to parks or gardens on their own, but they are often islands of tranquillity, perfect places in which to write a letter, picnic, watch people passing by, or just rest after a demanding tour or shopping expedition. Parks may also have special attractions like collections of rare plants, small zoos, branch museums, or puppet shows.

SCHOOLS. If your students have no homestay, they might still enjoy visiting a school, to compare it with their own and as a way of meeting other students. Write far in advance of your visit, to give the bureaucratic wheels a chance to turn. If you don't have the names of any schools or teachers, ask the consul or the cultural attaché at the country's embassy in Washington to give you some suggestions, or at least the address of the appropriate department of education.

HISTORICAL MUSEUMS. Many American students have only a very hazy idea of the histories of other countries. Artifacts—armor, clothing, household objects, weapons, documents—catch their imagination and their interest as no recitation of facts can do. If you can steer them toward particular objects that are relevant to places you've visited or things you've talked about, so much the better.

PERFORMING ARTS. Theater is a wonderful experience if the students' comprehension of the language is adequate for the play. Music and dance transcend language barriers; even students who don't go to such performances at home can enjoy ballet, opera, and concerts (classical, folk, or pop), because of their novelty and spectacle. Folk dance performances, with their lively pace, cheerful costumes, and pleasant music, appeal especially to students.

BANKS AND STOCK EXCHANGES. Students whose knowledge of banking and finance is limited to checking accounts, savings accounts, and personal loans can learn a lot by visiting a stock exchange or the foreign exchange department of an international bank. Brattleboro students were amazed at the Geneva stock exchange: the sight of 17 men shouting out bids as one man called the name of each stock gave them a dramatic introduction to high finance. Like the school visit, a tour of the bank or stock exchange should be arranged well in advance.

OPEN-AIR MARKETS. Farmer's markets, flea markets, and regular open-air markets offer not only local color, but also the possibility of bargains.

CHURCHES. Religious settings take on new richness in an unfamiliar language and setting. On one trip to Montreal, everyone in our group—Catholic, Protestant, and miscellaneous—benefited from Sunday Mass in the cathedral.

ART MUSEUMS AND GALLERIES. Out of curiosity or a sense of duty, students will generally find their way to the main art museum wherever they go—the Louvre or the Prado or the Kunsthistorisches Museum. They may also appreciate your guiding them to other museums and galleries: the specialization and smaller size of these put them on a more human scale; a visitor can see everything on one visit without feeling overwhelmed and finally numbed by sensory overload.

FACTORIES. It's fascinating to see raw materials being transformed into a finished product. Blocks of cedar are turned and enameled to become pencils; blocks of metal are punched out, complex mechanisms are added in dustless workrooms, and the finished watches are checked and rechecked before they leave the factory; vats of cocoa mixture are dripped, layer by layer, into forms on a conveyor belt that delivers the chocolates to a machine that wraps each one individually. Some factories routinely arrange tours for student groups as part of their public relations efforts; others refuse all such requests. If possible, write ahead; if not, leave room in your schedule for one such visit and when you arrive, ask the local Chamber of Commerce or tourist bureau for help.

GOVERNMENTAL OR INTERNATIONAL ORGANIZATIONS. Your students might like to visit a legislative session, a mint, your country's embassy in the foreign country, or the headquarters of an international organization. For example, the Red Cross staff showed our students films about the organization's relief work and its system for tracing refugees. Guidebooks can give you ideas for visits and details about hours and reservations.

SCAVENGER HUNT. You can write miscellaneous questions about the place the group is visiting and send out the students, individually or in teams, to get the answers. Offer a prize for finishing the hunt first, or for correctly answering the most questions in a set time. It might be easier to wait until you're there to make up the questions, though you'd then have to find a way to make multiple copies. The questions could demand that the students get information by talking with people, if their language is up to it; or the questions could simply require them to find their way around or get information from signs.

Some possible questions to get you started:

- How much does a local phone call cost?
- What's the address of the post office nearest the hotel?
- How does one get there from the hotel?
- What's the entry fee at the history museum?
- What is the name of a local newspaper?
- What American newspapers or magazines are widely available?
- Describe a mail carrier's uniform.
- How much is a movie ticket? Is there a discount for students?
- What's the name of the mayor of the town?
- What's the symbol for a pharmacy?
- What cultural events are going on on a given evening?
- How did you find out?
- Name a local brand of cigarette.
- How much does a loaf of bread cost?
- How much does a pair of American jeans cost?
- What time are religious services held at a given church?
- What is the name of————(a bridge, or mountain, or park), and why was it named that?

Evening activities

Evening activities during a homestay should take the host families into account, since evening may be the only time the whole family can be together and the families may count on spending that time with their guests. When your group isn't staying with families, evening activities should be things the group can do together, as you may want to be with them. They should know what the group will be doing, so they won't do the same thing beforehand and then plead to go off on their own at night.

Activities could include:

- Movies;

- Performances: music, dance, theater;

- Discos (though the students may be too young). Cover-charges or mandatory drinks (alcoholic or not) can be very expensive; check before you go.

- Seeing the city by night—from the water if it's on a body of water, from the top of a tall building, even by bus or on foot.

- Sports events.

If the hotel is in a fairly safe neighborhood and there are cafés or game rooms nearby, you could leave the students free to go off on their own, within limits (e.g., they can go one block in each direction, or two blocks on a certain street only, or whatever seems prudent; a sensible rule of thumb is that if you need to, you'll be able to locate them within ten or fifteen minutes). Set the limits, let them know you might be checking, and then do it—casually, in a friendly way, but showing them that you take your responsibility for them seriously.

Try to vary the evening activities, too, but don't feel apologetic about leaving a few blanks and expecting the students to stay in on those nights; if the days are full, the students will need some time to catch up with themselves, each other, their journals, and the hundreds of postcards they want to write—not to mention their sleep. They'll want to be out and about every night until they're ready to drop, but if you allow it, you'll soon find it hard to get them moving in the morning; the ones who did go to bed early and get up early will have to wait around, and tempers will begin to fray on all sides. If you can be firm and clear in your expectations from the outset, everyone will be happier in the end.

5

Keep in Touch with Your Counterpart

Don't assume anything—except goodwill

It's essential that you and the leader in your homestay community know what each other's responsibilities are; in order to define those responsibilities, you'll need to ask and answer a lot of specific questions. Because your counterpart is an adult, and probably a teacher, it's tempting to take his understanding and agreement for granted. Resist that temptation. Cultural differences, nuances of language, your two different personalities, and the vagaries of the international postal system will make communication hard enough. It's time-consuming to spell out a lot of very basic questions, but doing so can avoid confusion and hurt feelings on both sides. You can depend on the goodwill of everyone involved in the trip or exchange, but you and they can only act on that goodwill if you understand each other.

Although I'll put the questions mainly in terms of your trip abroad, you and your counterpart should settle the same questions for his group if they will return your visit as part of an exchange.

How are the participants chosen?

In a one-way trip this question may be of only marginal importance. If all the counterparts are in the same class at school, communication among your students will be easier than if they're scattered among different classes or different schools. Furthermore, families whose children are in the same class may work together to coordinate your stay better than families who don't know each other at all. Still, in a one-way trip the essential thing is that each student get along well with his or her family, and vice versa. How well the families work together doesn't concern you directly.

Still, compatibility—in personality, interests, and level of sophistication—will help any pair of counterparts get along, so trying to match the counterparts along these lines is worthwhile. It's especially important that the two groups be similar in their level of sophistication: even if students have the same chronological age, one group may be much more mature socially than the other. A group of blasé, worldly-wise 16-year-olds may look down on and resent their naive counterparts, while the less sophisticated group may become bewildered and perhaps resentful too.

If there's time to try to match individuals in a systematic way, the questionnaire in Chapter 6 will probably be helpful. Students on both sides should fill out similar questionnaires, and then one leader should send copies to the other, along with any supplementary information drawn from interviews with the students. Don't send originals of the questionnaires; they might get lost. On the basis of all this information, the second leader can assign the pairs of counterparts.

The question of how students are chosen can affect an exchange more directly than a one-way trip. The answer may reveal the students' own reasons for taking part in the exchange, which will be smoother if students on both sides have similar goals. For example, if students on one side are chosen on a first-come, first-served basis, economic realities may mean that those who come first are simply the ones with the most money, and not necessarily the ones with the deepest interest in learning about the other country. On the other hand, if students are chosen according to their interest (however that's measured) or their academic qualifications, they may be very appreciative guests, but as hosts they may not be able to provide the accommodations or entertainment that their counterparts expect. Students will probably assume that their counterparts are taking part in the exchange for the same reasons they are; if the selection procedures or the students' motivations are very different on the two sides, both groups should be aware of the differences. So ask about your counterpart's group:

- How old are the students?

- What are the requirements for participation? Do the students have to demonstrate proficiency in English, or interest in learning it? How are their proficiency and interest tested?

- Is the exchange connected with a school program? If so, do they receive credit for participating? If not, what organization is sponsoring it?

- Do all the students go to the same school?

- Who decides which students will participate? If it's not the person who'll travel with them, at what point does that person come in? How is that person chosen?

- What orientation do the students go through in preparation for the trip? How often do they meet?

- What rules will they be expected to observe during the trip?

Who will organize the students' daily program?

The more help you have, the better. On the other hand, even if your counterpart offers to organize the whole stay, you'll help him or her immeasurably by suggesting things you think your group would like, at the same time emphasizing that they are only suggestions; if they're impractical, or if your hosts have made other plans, that's fine. Here is where openness and trust on both sides are important: if you feel free to make suggestions and your counterpart feels free to reject them, the discussion can help both of you learn a lot about the other's culture and way of thinking.

Who will accompany the students in their activities?

Unless your counterpart asks you to do something else (like speaking to a class, or paying an official visit) that would prevent you from participating in the activities with the group, you should be with them. How can you know what they're going through unless you go through it, too? Furthermore, your participation shows the students that the activity is important to you, and that fact builds up its importance for your students.

Where will you stay?

In the rush of finding homestays for the students, don't forget to figure out where *you'll* stay. Ask your counterpart frankly if he or she can find a host family for you, too. In many ways your counterpart himself is the obvious host, because the two of you will be working together so much anyway, but a full-time houseguest may be too heavy a burden, especially if your counterpart is working or raising a family as well as helping you. However, he or she may be able to find you a family by asking around among colleagues or the host families or in the community at large. If this doesn't work, ask your counterpart (if it seems appropriate) whether there are any guest-houses or families that would take you in as a paying guest; such a situation might be more pleasant as well as less expensive than a hotel. Of course, depending on your finances, where you are, and how long you're staying, a hotel may be within your means and you might welcome the freedom and tranquillity it offers.

How will you get around?

If you'll be living in a town or near convenient public transportation, getting from one place to another will be no problem. Fortunately, public transportation is much better in most countries than in the U.S., so you may not need to worry about it at all. But if you're in the countryside, and public transportation is infrequent or nonexistent, you'll have to make some arrangements ahead of time for getting where you'll need to go. Your hosts may offer to drive you, but unless they do, you shouldn't assume that they're willing or even able to help. You may have to borrow or rent a car during your stay, but be sure to nail down the details ahead of time, to avoid surprises.

Transportation will probably be a less serious problem for you when you're abroad than for foreign group leaders during the American side of an exchange. Unless they know your area, they may assume there's public transportation; if there's none, you'll have to help arrange something. Give them details! As Dan and I live in the country, eight miles from town, the Swiss chaperones had decided to rent a car for their three-week stay. When they arrived and found out that it would cost at least $200 per person, they decided against it;

they simply hadn't budgeted that much. So for most of the three weeks the five of us piled into our aging VW beetle—when Dan could fit us into his work schedule. Maybe we could have avoided this situation, which was no one's fault, if we'd been in closer touch beforehand: they could have budgeted that sum, or I could have looked harder for alternatives to their renting a car.

Will you stay in the homestay community the entire time?

I've known host leaders who've planned a full program for visiting groups of foreign students, only to be left with full responsibility for the visitors when the groups' leaders took off for someplace more exciting. Maybe you just can't pass up a chance to visit family or close friends while you're abroad, though your visit should be at a convenient time for your counterpart—and *everyone* (students, parents, school officials, and your counterpart) should approve your plans well in advance. But put off tourism for some other time, when you're not with students. Otherwise they would wonder why, if you thought homestays were so valuable, you weren't sticking around to help guide them through theirs. Besides, you'd leave your counterpart with the whole responsibility for smoothing the relationships between students and their host families. All parties would probably resent your absence.

If you too have a host family, and they plan a trip for and with you, the situation's a little more delicate. If the planned trip is at the same time that *all* the families are going somewhere (e.g., for a long weekend or a school vacation week), there's no reason for you not to go with your hosts, as long as the students know where to reach you in case of an emergency. On the other hand, if some students' families aren't going anywhere, it may be important for you to be with those students: you could plan some special activity that would ease their feeling that they're missing out on something.

Who will pay for what?

To avoid confusion and embarrassment, you and your counterpart should arrange well ahead of time exactly what the hosts and guests will pay for. Of course there's no rule: your decision may depend on whether your hosts will also be visiting you, how elaborate their plans are, and even the currency exchange rate.

EXCHANGES. The first time we went to Switzerland, the dollar was so weak in comparison to the Swiss franc that we Americans threw ourselves on the hospitality of the Swiss: they paid not only for all our excursions and group expenses, but also for our students' incidental expenses, except the most personal. In return, when they came to the U.S., we paid their expenses during their stay in Vermont, where our weak dollar had some purchasing power. Allowing the hosts to pay was both convenient and rewarding: it turned the visitors on each side from tourists into guests. We used the same system again during the second exchange, and I recommend it no matter what the currency exchange situation.

As you and your counterpart in an exchange are working out who will pay for what, here are some expenses to consider:

- **Group excursions.** Who will pay for the charter bus, the entrance fee to the castle, the ballet tickets, the ski rentals?

- **Daily transportation.** Should the Americans budget bus fare? Will the host families drive them? Who'll be responsible for transporting the foreign students during their American homestay?

- **Meals outside the home.** The schedule for either side of the exchange may call for the guests to eat at school, in town between activities, or on the road during an outing. Will the families provide money or a picnic lunch for those meals? We agreed that when the meal was part of the groups' program, the host family would provide it. If the student wanted to eat away from home for his own convenience, he would pay for his food.

- **Family activities or host-guest outings.** If both go to a movie or a disco, or the family goes skiing for the day, who'll pay the guest's admission fee? We left this up to the individual family and guest, with the understanding that whatever they worked out would be the arrangement for both sides of the exchange.

ONE-WAY TRIP. Will your students help pay for their room and board? If most families where you're going are so poor that they can't afford to receive another person into their homes, it may be in order for your students to contribute toward their room and board. The subject demands tact. If you think it appropriate, by all means discuss it with your counterpart, and especially if he or she has told you that families are eager to receive your students but simply can't afford to. On the other hand, your counterpart may be looking for a tactful way to say that enough families simply can't be found to take in your students. In any case, you should realize that if the students pay for their room and board, it will probably complicate the relationship between them and their families. There's no way to measure hospitality or how pleasant a guest someone is, so there's no objective way to know whether a given host-guest relationship is worth the money that changes hands—and yet both sides will be tempted to say, "This isn't worth it," or "What a good deal!" Even if both think it's a good deal, their relationship is to some degree a business deal as well as a meeting of two people—and if there are problems with the relationship, working them out will be more difficult because resentment will focus on the financial aspect of things: "I'm paying them, so why shouldn't I . . . ?" or, "We're being paid to provide room and board, not to . . . ." So if your students are paying for room and board, you'll need to emphasize, first to your counterpart and then to your students, how important it is that they be treated—and act— like members of the family and not like paying guests.

In a one-way trip, of course, it wouldn't be fair to expect families who are welcoming a foreign guest into their homes to incur any additional expenses. Therefore the visitors should plan to pay for everything except, perhaps, room and board: bus fare, snacks, movies and other entertainment, and any excursions they take or any additional group activities. It might be nice to include enough money in the budget so that each student could invite someone from his or her family to accompany the group on sightseeing visits you plan during the homestay. In addition, you might want to plan a party at the end of your stay to honor the host families. (For details on organizing such a party, see Chapter 13, "Help the Students Show Gratitude.")

Expectations

Other questions for your counterpart can help avoid misunderstandings and give your students a head start in learning about the country where you'll be going. For example, if you and your counterpart agree that students will be treated "like members of the family," what does that mean? Asking your counterpart for very specific information will help you prepare the students for their homestay. Some possible questions follow. If you can answer them already, based on your own travel experience, so much the better; you won't need to bother your counterpart with them.

- **Meals.** What time do most families eat? What is the main meal? Does the whole family usually eat together? Many American students, used to coming home late from extracurricular activities or work and eating on the run, are amazed to find that their host families eat together *every single day.*

- **What are the most common foods?**

- **Clothes.** Find out what the weather will probably be while you're there, whether students should bring very warm clothes, rain gear, or cool clothes. Students may not be aware of local conventions about dress: one American girl's French father refused to let her leave the house in shorts, and a Swiss girl horrified her host family and their friends by doffing the top of her bikini at the Brattleboro swimming pool. Ask your counterpart if there are any occasions in the program (sports events on the one hand, formal evenings on the other) that call for specialized or formal clothing.

- **Transportation of students.** Are the families concentrated in one area, or are they widely scattered? How will they get to a central meeting place? If, during the American side of an exchange, American students will be driving their guests, the visitors' parents should know that; they may not realize how much American families (including teenagers) depend on their cars.

- **Drinking.** Is it probable that families will serve wine or beer with meals? What part does alcohol play in social life among students?

- **Drugs.** Are drugs routinely available? Rarely available? Taboo? Which drugs might the students encounter?

- **Politics.** Knowing what political issues are most pressing in the host country will help your students feel comfortable there. Some of these questions (abortion, or nuclear disarmament) could sound familiar to American students, but they'll soon discover how such issues can vary from country to country. They may inform themselves about these questions or they may not, but at least they'll know what their hosts are talking about, and they may hold back from saying something rash themselves.

- **Social life.** What do students do for amusement? Do they go out in couples, or in groups, or both? Do they go to each others' houses for parties? Do they go into town? Will the families chaperone parties at home? Will they expect to know where the students are when they're not home? Will they set curfews? Will the families expect different things from boys and girls, or will they treat the two sexes alike?

Health

Your counterpart may be able to give you some useful information about health. Are there any diseases that are common in the host country that your students should know about? Should they get any inoculations, even though none may be required by authorities in either country? Do people customarily drink tap water? If not, is it because they don't consider it safe or because they prefer bottled water?

The more information your counterpart can give you about the homestay community and the families' expectations, the more easily you and your group will be able to adapt to the new situation. Of course, in an exchange you owe your counterpart the same kind of information about your community. Even if he or she is an experienced traveler, particular circumstances can vary a great deal from one part of the U.S. to another. Good intentions can go a long way, but they go even further when everyone knows what to expect.

6

Form Your Group and Get Moving

Now it's time to gather information about your students, decide (if you haven't yet done so) which ones will go, and help them begin their preparations for the trip.

Have students fill out applications—with medical information

If you have more interested students than places in the group, an application can help you decide which students will go. Even if you already know who'll be going, it's a good idea to draw up an application form to get some information on paper; unless you already know all the students very well indeed, you can't expect to keep a lot of details about each one in your head.

Of course you may already have distributed applications at some earlier point in the process of forming the group. The exact order of the steps in that process isn't important, as you've probably gathered by now; everyone involved with the trip needs information at various points along the way, and you gather information and disseminate it whenever it seems necessary and practical.

Here is a sample application form. The items marked with * are necessary only if the students are participating in an exchange rather than a one-way trip.

Application

Name _____ Age _____

Address _____

Home phone _____

Parents' names _____

How can parent(s) be reached when not at home?

Mother: Phone number(s) _____ hours _____

Father: Phone number(s) _____ hours _____

Are you taking any medication (Either regularly or from time to time, as with asthma or allergy medication)?

_____

Do you have any chronic physical problems? Describe them.

_____

Do you wear glasses? _____ If so, do you need them all the time, or for reading, or for seeing things at a distance? _____

Do you wear contact lenses? _____

Is there anything that a doctor should be aware of in treating you, if you are incapable of telling the doctor yourself?

_____

Do you have any allergies?_____ To what? _____

Do you have medication for your allergies? _____

Do you have any allergies that might require emergency action (e.g., an allergy to beestings)? _____

Who else lives with you? Please give ages of brothers or sisters.

_____

_____

*Do you have any pets? (Describe, in case your counterpart has allergies) _____

*Describe your home (city, country, house, apartment, etc.) _____

*Would your counterpart have his or her own room? _____

If not, whose room would he or she share? _____

*Must your family host a girl or a boy? _____

*Which would you prefer? _____

Do you smoke? _____

*Does your family have strong objections to hosting a student who smokes? _____

*How do you get to school? _____

*Will you have a driver's license and access to a car while your counterpart is here? _____

Please write out your school schedule on the back of this sheet.

Do you work? _____ Where? _____

How many hours per week? _____

*If you work, how will you provide for your counterpart while you're working?

_____

What extracurricular activities do you take part in?

_____

What are your other interests and activities outside of school?

_____

Why do you want to go on this trip?

_____

Where have you traveled? Who was with you?

_____

Describe yourself in a few phrases:

_____

Rate yourself in the following areas:

1	2	3	4	5

I usually see the   I'm very serious.
funny side of things.

1	2	3	4	5

I'm often forgetful   I'm very organized
or disorganized.   and responsible.

1	2	3	4	5

I'm very quiet.   I'm very outgoing.

1	2	3	4	5

Speaking (_____)   Speaking (_____)
comes easily to me.   is hard for me.

Please enclose letters from two adults (teachers, employers, family, friends) recommending you for this trip.

We have read the Conditions of Participation and agree to them and to the participation of the undersigned student in this experience.

Parent _____ Date _____

Participant _____ Date _____

Obviously, this application goes into a lot of detail. Some of the information is necessary in case of an emergency (you can detach the first sheet and take it with you when you go, as a record for each student), and some of it is necessary in order to match students with their counterparts; the rest just helps you get to know each student. Of course, your destination, the kind of trip, and the particular circumstances will determine exactly what questions you will ask in the application: for example, some areas may require or recommend special immunization shots; the form could ask when they were administered, although you may need further proof of immunization as well.

You may want to tell students that they can add information to this sheet after their parents have signed it; girls may be taking oral contraceptives without their parents' knowledge.

Letters of recommendation not only acquaint you with the students, but also give adults outside the students' families an interest in their successful participation in the trip.

Meet the students individually

Application in hand, you can meet with each student to go over it. I used the occasion to check on some routine matters (e.g., how far along each one was in the process of getting a passport) and to establish a friendly, one-to-one relationship. I asked some fairly personal questions about their strengths and weaknesses, telling the students that by being open they could help me plan our orientation sessions.

At the same time I outlined my expectations, telling the students frankly that in order for the trip to be a success, each student would have to take a lot of responsibility for himself or herself, and would also have to be very sensitive to the other people in the group.

During this first interview, it can also be useful to go over each student's academic load and extracurricular commitments, to help fit orientation meetings and fund raising among the student's other obligations. It's helpful to have a school calendar handy, so that actors will know that they won't be around for the musical, and athletes will realize that they'll miss the playoffs—it's nearly impossible to schedule a trip around *all* extracurricular activities. Students should also begin planning right away to keep up with their schoolwork in any classes they'll miss (see "Help students prepare for schoolwork they'll miss," this chapter).

We filled out a form on each student, so we would have a record later: after 10 or more interviews, any one student's reactions are hard to remember. Here is a sample form:

Echange avec la Suisse

Individual conference

Student's name _____ Date of conference _____

Passport: __ in hand __ sent for __ birth certificate sent for __ photos taken

Contact with Swiss partner: __ no __ yes: When? _____ What? _____

Courses you will be taking during the trip:

Course name   *Comments*

_____

_____

_____

_____

_____

_____

Extracurricular commitments: _____

_____

What are you looking forward to most?

What are you looking forward to least?

What do you hope to gain from this experience?

What strengths do you bring to the group and/or the experience?

Test students' foreign-language skills

If it's appropriate, you can also check each student's communicative skills in the host country's language at this time. Keep the testing as simple as possible. Taping the tests makes it easy to compare them to each other, and they can also serve as pretests if you want to measure the students' progress during the preparation and the trip. A simple test could consist of:

- **Pictures:** one showing someone who obviously doesn't feel well, one of someone who's obviously lost; other action pictures; one of a clock showing the time, one illustrating an expression about the weather. You'll need eight pictures in all.

- **A cue sheet for the evaluator.** Cues can be varied:

  1. Greet the student, who should respond appropriately.

  2. Ask the student's name.

  3. Show the picture of the person who doesn't feel well; ask, "What is wrong?"

  4. Show another picture; ask, "What's going on here?"

  5. Show another picture; ask, "Where is . . . ?"

  6-10. Indicate that for the final five pictures, the *student* should ask an appropriate question.

- **A rating sheet for each student.**

Name _____

	0	1	2	3		General Comments
1.						
2.						
3.						
4.						
5.						
6.						
7.						
8.						
9.						
10.						

For each question, the evaluator rates each student 0 (no response), 1 (inappropriate response), 2 (appropriate response, but with errors), or 3 (appropriate response, error-free). The evaluator should move quickly through the questions, making the ratings as inconspicuously as possible. The five final questions are more open-ended; any appropriate questions can be acceptable.

This sort of test is quite simple, and can help you sort out which students can understand and express themselves easily, and which ones have problems. Two things to watch out for: the pictures should have enough going on in them so that they won't confound students for lack of a single vocabulary item, and the evaluator must be consistent. An appropriate answer from one student is an appropriate answer from another student, even if one has studied the language for much longer than the other.

Record students' preparations

A chart will help you keep track of when your students complete each step of the preparation—from handing in their preliminary permission forms to getting their passports to writing to their homestay families.

	meeting with parents 9/25	preliminary permission form	individual interview	orientation meeting 10/10	car wash 10/14	project idea	passport applied for	passport obtained	wrote first letter to host family	orientation meeting 10/24
Pete Panetti	✓	9/26	10/4	✓	✓	10/12	10/18	11/4	✓	✓
Irene Bryan	✓	10/1	10/2	✓	sick	10/16	10/20	11/9		
Janie Tole	✓	9/30	10/6	exc.	✓	10/22	already has	✓	✓	✓

Help your students get passports and international student I.D.'s

No matter where the group is going, with the exception of Canada, it's very helpful for each student to have a passport. Even when one isn't absolutely necessary for crossing the border, a passport is universally recognized as proof of identity: a bank teller or bureaucrat will accept it when a birth certificate or driver's license could lead to confusion and delay. Students should apply for a passport well ahead of your departure date. They may need time to assemble all the necessary materials before sending or taking their application to a passport office: they may have to wait for an official birth certificate to be sent from wherever they were born, or until they get the correct number of copies of the correct kind of photo.

International student identity cards can entitle students to student rates and discounts. Furthermore, according to the *New York Times* (April 1, 1984), the cards automatically include accident and sickness insurance. They are available for a modest fee from:

> The Council on International
> Educational Exchange
> 205 E. 42nd Street
> New York, New York 10017

Circulate a letter to the faculty

Explaining your trip in detail to your colleagues will help enlist their cooperation. Your students will need their teachers' help if they'll be missing classes, and you may need help if you'll be trying to arrange classes for visitors in an exchange.

In your letter, tell teachers what the students will be doing during the trip and the dates when you'll be gone; attach a list of the students involved. For an exchange, give the dates of the foreign students' visit, especially if it falls in the school year.

Above all, emphasize the students' obligation to keep up with their classwork, and ask the teachers to help them fulfill that obligation. Teachers can help by giving the students their work well ahead of time, if possible: students might be able to complete some of their assignments before they leave. You could suggest that some teachers assign work that's connected with the trip: an English teacher might require students to keep a daily journal, or a social studies teacher might ask students to prepare an oral or written report on geographical, historical, sociological, or economic aspects of the host country. It's important that the teachers' expectations be realistic: the students will be spending most of their time and energy struggling to understand what they're seeing and hearing, so the most successful assignments will be based on their personal experiences, not on academic research.

If you've scheduled some study time into the group's program, let their teachers know that, and if they'll have time during a homestay to do schoolwork, say that, too. And finally, if the students must complete projects about some aspect of the United States to present to classes or groups while they're abroad, be sure to tell your colleagues about the projects: they may be able to give your students some suggestions or advice. (For details about these projects, see "Help students develop projects," this chapter.)

Help students prepare for schoolwork they'll miss

No matter what arrangements students make with their teachers for catching up on work they miss, it might be a good idea to draw up a contract form to get those arrangements down in writing. The form should have places to indicate what work is to be done, when it must be completed, how it will be graded, and what proportion of the student's final grade it will represent. Distribute blank contracts to each student for all their subjects; when the student and the teacher have agreed on the student's responsibilities, both can sign the contract, which you can then file. If a student has no obligations in a given course, the teacher can just write "NONE" on the contract and sign it.

Of course in the end the students alone are responsible for making up their work, but you can help by providing the contract forms and checking them as they come in, just as you check whether the students have their passports.

If there are guidance counselors or faculty advisors in your school to help students carry out their academic responsibilities, call on these people for help. You may want their advice before you write up any contracts, or you may want to turn the contracts over to them for follow-up.

Encourage students to write to their counterparts

When students have their counterparts' names and addresses, they'll find that writing to them will establish friendships before they even meet. Your students may be shy or nervous about writing, but you can help them by simultaneously insisting that they write, and offering to help them individually in any way you can—providing vocabulary, if the counterparts speak another language, or suggesting what to write.

If students will be communicating with their homestay families in another language, I require them to write at least the first letter in that language. It's important that the families have an idea of their guests' competence in their language. A letter may give a better indication than how long a student has "taken" the language at school.

The first letter could include basic information about the student: for example, her age, a description of her family and where she lives, her interests and hobbies. It's nice to send a photo or two, especially snapshots: students on both sides are interested not only in their counterparts as individuals, but also in the context in which those individuals live. Houses, landscapes, and activities forming the background in photos help students imagine their counterparts' daily lives.

Host families appreciate knowing that their guests are eager to begin the trip, but students may neglect to mention their enthusiasm, since it seems so evident to them. You may want to suggest some appropriate ways for them to express their eagerness. The expression that comes most naturally to them seems to be, "I'm very excited about the trip;" a literal translation could be ambiguous, because "excited" has so many meanings, and many dictionaries fail to distinguish among them. Tactfully explaining the ambiguity and providing suitable alternative expressions for your students can save them needless embarrassment.

Once they've established contact by mail, it's important for them to maintain it. This need not mean a series of long letters. Postcards of your area, or greeting cards for birthdays and holidays, will let the counterparts know that your students are thinking of them and will also provide the cultural context I mentioned earlier. How often they write is more important than how much they write.

Help students develop projects

This idea originated with Bob Schermer, a German teacher, whose students at South Burlington High School participate in an exchange with German students. In our second Swiss exchange, each American student (sometimes working with a partner) prepared a very short talk, lasting from three to five minutes, on some aspect of Vermont or of American life. The students looked up the French vocabulary they needed in order to talk about their subjects, and they prepared audio-visual materials ranging from maps and tourist brochures to tapes and live demonstrations. The students came up with the topics themselves, so the projects generally reflected their interests and extracurricular activities. They included:

- our school's marching band (with pictures and newspaper clippings);
- making maple syrup (with a diagram to show the flow of sap into the boiler; the girl who presented this had helped her grandparents make maple syrup on their farm);
- elections in the U.S. (with pictures and materials for an overhead projector);
- sports: one on professional basketball, one on high school soccer;
- tourist attractions in Vermont (with maps and brochures);
- a talk about the Big Brother/Big Sister program by two girls who had "little sisters" through the program;

- the Fourth of July;
- baton twirling (with a live demonstration; the girl took her baton to Switzerland just for the presentation);
- folk dance in Vermont (with pictures and a tape of contra–dance music).

I sent a list of students and their projects to M. Troesch, who circulated it among the teachers at the Swiss counterparts' schools. As a result, most students were invited to give their presentations to at least one class—often an English class, which was a relief to the students, some of whom were very nervous about speaking French in front of a group. Most of them ended up speaking French anyway as they answered questions, since the Swiss were more comfortable asking the questions in French.

The projects served several purposes at once: they made the students try to see at least one thing in their everyday lives from the foreign point of view, and they made them explain that thing in terms their hosts could understand; they gave the students confidence about speaking French; they made each student the legitimate center of attention at a given moment and integrated the Americans into their classes in Geneva; finally, and most importantly, they provided springboards for questions and conversation between American and Swiss students—conversation that ranged far beyond the projects' necessarily limited topics. Marge Yoder later wrote about her project,

> It went OK, but we never exactly finished it. We got about halfway finished and they started asking about other things. They were more interested in Americans in general than in marching bands.

Jeff Record (who talked about New York City) said people wanted to know:

> Is there a big drug problem in the U.S.? Do people watch a lot of TV? Are the meals different? Does your mother work? What's the average working day like?

These sorts of questions are useful because they make the students reflect on the "American way of life" in its variety and complexity, and on the differences between the supercharged images that other cultures have of the U.S. and the students' own daily lives. The hosts' questions also reveal a great deal about *their* culture, so your students can learn from their hosts at the same time that they're helping them learn about the U.S. The projects serve as catalysts in this interchange of growing curiosity and insight.

You may want your students to do a totally different sort of project, particularly if they would not have the opportunity to present a project on the U.S. during their travel abroad: you may wish them to prepare a project on some aspect of the place or places you visit, so that when they return to your school and community from their travel they will have, literally, something to show for it. The project could involve research on the background of one of the sites you visit; it could consist of interviews with people who live in the host country on some topic; it could be a photo-essay on a specific site or theme. The possibilities are endless, especially when the students feel free to come up with their own ideas.

They may need you to help them define the scope of their projects, since ambitious students tend to take on topics that are much too broad, and lazy ones are sometimes satisfied with a brief and superficial glance at a topic. The purpose is to give them a window on their experience—not to produce research papers. They will appreciate your interest, which will encourage them to put some time and effort into their presentations; you can also help them figure out a lively format for presenting whatever information they have gathered.

7

Public Relations

Why bother?

Travel for students seems to bring out kindly interest in nearly everyone. At times the adult world seems divided between people who have traveled and want young people to have the same opportunity, and people who've never traveled and want young people to have the chance they missed. Both groups take a generous, vicarious interest in the students' travel and go out of their way to make it easier—and even to make it possible.

You will probably be calling on all these people for help. Your group may ask merchants, organizations and individuals for all kinds of support. You may sell them things they don't need, like raffle tickets or booster buttons; you may ask them to donate goods or services as raffle prizes; you may ask them to lend equipment for a carwash. They may even be members of the school board who vote to authorize the trip. In any case, they'll probably be willing to help out if they know something about what you're doing. If they've read an artical in the newspaper, heard a radio talk-show about your trip, or seen a poster, they feel involved, and your group can make the most of this feeling. Getting people outside the school involved in what you're doing by letting them know about it is the essence of public relations.

Good publicity also has indirect benefits. The trip can be the best possible advertising for your school or organization. For example, if drama students are committed enough to go to England to see plays, they must be learning something in English classes. If foreign language students can live with families who don't speak English, they must be learning the language well and feel enthusiastic about learning more.

Good publicity encourages the students themselves. They'll be happy to be going, of course, but they'll be even happier when other people know about the trip. On the one hand, all the fuss makes them feel important; on the other, it can make them more sensitive. When people tell them, "You're so lucky. I wish I could go!" or "I never had the chance to do that when I was in school. We had to stick with exercises in books," students are less inclined to take the trip for granted. They sometimes even begin to see themselves as representatives of their school, their town, or their country.

Whether or not you try to generate good publicity, anything that goes seriously wrong on the trip will be in the public eye. It will be NEWS, and you'll have very little control over the news. You'll be glad that you managed to establish a positive impression in people's minds before problems arose.

Getting started

Before you take the first steps to publicize your group, check with your supervisor. Often administrators are glad to have teachers take the initiative because the good impression that's created reflects well on the entire school and, by extension, on the administrators themselves. The school may have a specific procedure you'll have to follow, or it may even have a policy that discourages teachers from making contact with the media on their own.

Some schools have their own public-relations staff—either a full-time professional, or a teacher who does public relations work for the school on the side. Find out what help is available at your school; there's no reason why you should take on these tasks yourself if someone in the school system is paid to do them. Still, no one knows what your trip involves as well as you and your students do, so you should be ready to give the public relations person the information you'd like the public to have.

Newspapers

Talk to people at your newspaper

Local newspapers exist to let people know what's going on in their own communities, so use yours. Call either the editor or the school reporter and explain what your group is doing. If you live in a large urban or suburban area, by all means talk with people at the big newspapers that serve your area, but don't neglect smaller, neighborhood papers. You want to reach people who might get involved.

Different editors see "news" differently. For some, a strawberry supper to raise funds for your trip is news, and they'll gladly print a story for each of your fund-raising activities. Other editors insist on "hard" news—stories about an important event that has already happened. Some editors may be willing to run announcements of fund-raising events in a column listing such activities, while others will insist on a full-fledged article. It's up to you to fit the information you want printed to the policy of each paper.

Editors also have different ways of getting the news. If you're lucky, an experienced reporter will interview you and/or your students, in person or on the phone, and write a detailed article. The editor may expect you to write the article yourself, and provide photographs too. Whether you're writing an article yourself, or providing information to a reporter, the results will be better if you follow a few guidelines.

What are you trying to say?

Are you giving information about a specific activity? Do people already know something about your trip? If not, can you sum it up briefly so they will have the background they need?

Be specific

Help people form visual images of what you are describing. If you're promoting a raffle, list some of the most attractive prizes; if you're explaining what the students' trip will be like, name some of the sights you expect to see.

Vague	Specific
The group has gathered a lot of good prizes from area merchants.	Elywn's Furniture has donated a maple candle stand, and Aiken's Hardware contributed an ice chest.

Avoid passive constructions

To put it another way, "Passive constructions are to be avoided by the writer." They are flabby and dull. Use strong verbs, and use them strongly: telling who does what makes it more real for the reader.

Passive	Active
A lot of time and effort has been given to this dance, and it's hoped that a good time will be had.	Andrea Gorman and her committee have worked hard on this dance, so all of us in the group hope people will have a good time.

Name names

I learned this lesson from my students. A colleague interviewed me about our exchange with Switzerland, and I tried to give interesting details of the various things we'd done to prepare for the trip, and the students' reactions. I didn't mention individual students by name because I didn't want to leave anyone out. Wrong decision! When the long, detailed article was printed, all the students eagerly looked for their names or their friends' names—and of course they were all disappointed. It's better to mention some students' names (making sure, of course, that the anecdotes won't embarrass them) than to try to be scrupulously fair by not mentioning any.

Ask the editor for suggestions

If you're going to write any articles yourself, the editor may have very specific guidelines concerning the general format of the article or details of style. There may be a stylebook that reporters at that paper use as a reference and that you, too, can use. If you've never done any of this sort of work, *News Writing for Non-Professionals,* by W.C. Line (Nelson-Hall, 1979) is a good general guide.

Start with a strong lead

Keep in mind the "Who? What? When? Where? Why?" of traditional journalism, and try to answer at least some of those questions in your opening paragraph, so the reader will know where he is right away. At the same time try to plant a "hook," some intriguing detail that will involve the reader and force him to go on to the rest of the story in order to satisfy his curiosity.

Standard

This spring the Plattville German Club will go to Hamburg, Germany, for two weeks.

In Hamburg the members of the club will stay with German families . . .

Livelier

In early April, as his friends celebrate the start of Easter vacation, Joe Rankin will celebrate Easter with his German homestay family.

Members of the Plattville German Club, Joe and 16 other students will stay with families . . .

or even:

In early April, Joe Rankin will be able to say, "I am a Hamburger."

Joe and 16 of his fellow members of the Plattville German Club will stay with families in the West German city of Hamburg as part of . . .

Put important information first

Readers are impatient, and newspaper writers must allow for this impatience by putting the main message at the beginning of the article. If the reader moves on before finishing the story he will have at least the main idea.

A general format for your articles could be as follows:

Lead . . . . as above (for this particular article)

Main idea . . . . students are about to leave on their trip

Expand on main idea . . . . their feelings; details about what they'll be doing during the trip; school authorities' comments

Background . . . . how the trip got started; what the group has done so far

Use quotes and short paragraphs

One important difference between newspaper stories and magazine articles or books is their layout. Newspaper stories are usually laid out in narrow columns, though editors will sometimes give feature articles a double-column layout. Long paragraphs, no matter how interesting, come out on the newspaper page as long, unbroken blocks of type, and a reader finds them much more forbidding than the same information arranged in smaller units. Short paragraphs give the reader's eyes—and his mind—a break.

Quotes can help break up the text, since each quote is a new paragraph. They also give human feelings, expressed in a human voice, to the information in the article. You can abandon the detached tone of a reporter and draw readers into the experience you're reporting if you quote individuals who are involved in that experience.

It's important that people you want to quote know that you'll be quoting them. Ask them directly: "May I quote you in the article I'm writing?" Take notes in order to capture their particular way of expressing themselves, since it's their individual voices that will enliven your story. You don't need to worry about quoting them absolutely word for word: you can change the order of their sentences, as long as you don't distort their meaning, or you can leave out parts of sentences if they're redundant. The person should *never* be able to say about a quote, "I never said that." If you got only the gist of what someone said, you can use indirect quotes. If you take careful notes, you'll avoid that dilemma.

One way to get a story about some aspect of the trip is to sit down with a group of students, ask them some questions that will lead toward the information you hope to convey, and note their responses.

No quotes	**Quotes**
. . . The students are certainly looking forward to their trip, although they expressed some nervousness about living with a family that speaks very little English.	. . . "Just 20 more days!" said Christine Murray. "Every day I wake up and think, 'Wow, pretty soon we'll really be there!'" Some students are a little nervous. "It seems dumb, but I can't imagine just speaking Spanish from morning till night," said Mickey Talmadge . . .

Ask someone to look it over

If you're nervous about the article, ask someone with writing experience to help you check it. A journalism teacher or someone who writes regularly would be the obvious choices, but if you can't locate a professional, then ask anyone who is comfortable with writing and who will tell you honestly whether you've written what you intended. Seek out a colleague who will take the time to look at the article carefully and who will be forthright about suggesting improvements. It isn't very helpful if someone skims it, hands it back and says "Sure, it looks fine to me."

Here are some questions you and the person helping you can ask as you read over the article together:

- What's the most important information you want to convey?

- Is that information clear, and near the beginning of the article?

- To whom are you addressing the story? To the general public? Students? Your colleagues? The school board?

- Do you give the background information your audience will need?

- Does the article move quickly and smoothly from start to finish? If there are awkward spots, did you jump too quickly from one thing to another, leaving out information, or did you get bogged down in details you should leave out? Or could rearranging the information make the article flow more smoothly?

Photographs

Pictures that accompany an article about your group should show something about the group's activities. Too many newspaper photos of clubs or civic organizations are nothing but group portraits: under a shot of six people staring into the camera, the caption reads, "The newly elected officers of the Greater Centerville Civic Club include (from left) . . ." Action—almost any action—is better than none. If your students are selling bumper stickers, take a picture of the principal sticking one on her car; it will show that the administration supports your group. If they have a pie sale, get a shot of them baking or selling pies; it will show that they're willing to work for their trip, and that the public is involved. When you can, include a sign or logo or foreign flag in the picture to distinguish your group from all the others that sell pies, hold raffles, get on buses to go on trips, etc.

Editors should specify what sort of picture they require. They will almost certainly demand black-and-white originals, as color shots often look strange reprinted in black and white on newsprint. Some editors accept Polaroid originals; some actually prefer them; some insist on prints of 35 mm film, which they will crop to fit the available space; some want negatives, which they will have printed at the paper to suit their needs.

Two technical suggestions: first, try to keep the photo simple. A clear photo of only a few students, showing what they're doing, is much more forceful and interesting than a long shot of the whole group, who will be reduced to small fuzzy spots. Secondly, aim for strong contrast in the print, as contrasty photos reproduce much better than shades of gray.

Radio and Television

Local radio and television coverage can reach people who don't read local newspapers, and it can reinforce the involvement of those who do.

Talk with the station manager

The station manager can tell you whether the station might give air time to publicize your group's activities, and if so, what form the coverage could take. Perhaps you can make public service announcements, 30- or 60-second tapes describing what your group is doing. Your departure, your arrival back home, or the activities you've arranged for your foreign guests might merit local news coverage; your students or your foreign guests could take part in a talk show. While we were in Switzerland, one radio station at home arranged for a long-distance phone call, which it broadcast live early in the morning. Another exchange group used cable TV to raise money for their trip (see "Organize an Auction," Chapter 8).

Talk shows

Radio and TV talk shows give your students a fine chance to tell people why they're taking part in the trip and what they're getting out of it. If you have foreign guests, talk shows offer other people in the community a chance to share the discoveries and insights of your guests.

If you, your students, or your guests are on a talk show, it helps ease everyone's

nervousness to get together for a few minutes beforehand. The moderator may be there, too, but even if she doesn't have time to do that preliminary work with the group, she'll appreciate their having given some thought to what they want to say; she may be able to give them an idea of some of the questions she'll ask. Ask the students which aspects of the trip they want to discuss; suggest ideas you think are important; help them think of ways to make transitions from one subject to another.

Just as in a newspaper article, lively details make the experience more real to the audience. What are the students looking forward to the most? What are they doing to get ready? What is the group as a whole doing? What are they a little nervous about? If they've already been, what is their favorite memory? Were there any surprises? What questions did people ask them?

A caution: on radio and TV it's better *not* to talk about other people by name, unless it's someone who did something specific for the group (for example, a merchant who donated something, or someone who helped with orientation). When you say something on radio or TV, you can't take it back. Even if the production is being taped for later broadcast, it's often hard, or even impossible, to edit indiscretions. Apologizing or trying to cover up a slip doesn't usually help. Caution students to think carefully before mentioning anything that happened to someone else, to be sure that the person wouldn't be embarrassed— and not to mention any names, just in case.

One of my students described our group's visit to Paris on a live radio show:

> Our hotel was in a good neighborhood. But ———, who graduated
> from the high school last year, invited us all to her apartment, and it was kind
> of scary, because the neighborhood was pretty bad.

Realizing how that might sound, she tried to make amends:

> —Um, I don't mean that she lived in a slum or anything; Mrs. Cassidy
> told us that apartments in good neighborhoods are really expensive.

If members of our Paris hostess's family were listening, they took it well; the moderator invited listeners to call in, and although we had several calls, we didn't hear from them.

Take the Show on the Road

Particularly when you return from the trip, some of the students will probably be eager to share their experiences with interested listeners. Putting together a presentation is a good way to thank organizations that helped you, or to build support for the next trip, or simply to give your students an outlet for their enthusiasm.

Get an invitation

Call or write to any groups in your community who might be interested in a slide show or panel discussion. Some possibilities are:

- the school board
- the parent-teacher organization
- senior-citizens' groups, nursing homes
- the Chamber of Commerce

- the Elks, Lions, Rotary, Kiwanis, Jaycees, etc.
- religious groups
- clubs interested in international issues
- women's groups
- Scout troops, 4-H clubs
- groups or classes in the school itself

Ask the contact person for the organization how many students should come, how long their presentation should take, and what aspects of the trip might hold particular interest for the members of that organization.

Plan your presentation

If slides are the backbone of the presentation, students should choose pictures that have special importance to them. They should put the slides in some logical order, avoiding duplication, and prepare a comment on each slide, explaining why they chose it.

Many students take color prints, rather than slides. If they mount the photos on a big sheet of stiff cardboard, with a caption for each print, the display can accompany a panel discussion. Each student can prepare part of the display, or they can work together. It needn't be very elaborate; a general title, like "Memories of Mexico," can cover everyone's favorite pictures.

A group of students simply talking about their travels with an interested audience can be the best possible public relations for your trip. The Windham World Affairs Council, a group of adults interested in international questions, invited six of our high-school students to speak at the Council's annual dinner. Two students had been to Mexico for a two-week homestay, two had taken part in an exchange with German students, and two had stayed with Swiss families for almost three weeks. My department chairman, Al Lynch, and I, who were to serve as moderators, met with the students and the woman planning the program. We agreed to begin with the following questions:

- What did you expect before you went?
- What surprises did you have when you got to the other country?
- Did you see things about the other country's way of life that you admired and would like to see here?
- Did you see the U.S. differently after your trip?
- What questions did people ask you about the U.S.?

Once the students got over their initial nervousness, their fresh perceptions and their enthusiasm caught up even the most seasoned travelers in the audience. Kathy talked about dating customs in her Mexican family; Calico praised the honor system on public buses in Geneva; Melissa lamented Americans' lack of interest in foreign languages; and Ted observed that many Germans seemed to know more about American history than he did. Listening to them talk, I understood how much students can learn from foreign travel—far more than even we, their teachers, usually realize.

Other Ideas

Design a logo

A logo will help identify your group in the public's memory. Ask for volunteers among the students to design a logo for the group. It can be as simple as some combination of the American flag and that of the country you're going to visit, or it can be an elaborate design representing your region, landmarks of the place you're visiting . . . the possibilities are endless.

Print up material

Ask local merchants to display posters ("We Support the Podunk Drama Club Trip") or programs of the visitors' stay to show their backing for your activity. Bumper stickers, lapel buttons, or small stickers serve the same purpose. These items cost money, but perhaps a printer or merchant will provide them. Thank whoever donates the material by printing on it, if there's room, "Donated by ———."

Leaflets which briefly explain the origin and purpose of the trip or exchange can spare you and your students a lot of repetitive explanations. The leaflets can be very simple: a dittoed sheet or even a half-sheet will do fine. Decorate it with the group's logo and make it available at all your fund–raising activities. Be sure to include someone's name and phone number (a willing parent's or your own) so people who wish to help the group in some way can get in touch with you.

Put displays in public places

Arrange with a photography shop, another merchant, a bank, or the public library for your group to set up a display, either in the window or in the building itself. The students can include souvenirs as well as maps, flags, and brochures to accompany photos they took. Be sure to label each photo or at least each group of photos, as well as the display itself.

Declare "Foreign Trip Week"

Arrange with the local government (the mayor, the city council, or whoever is in charge of such things) to proclaim "British Drama Day" on the date of your departure for England, or "Foreign Study Week" while your group is in Italy. The authorities are especially likely to agree to these schemes if they already know about your activities. If foreign visitors will be coming to your community as part of an exchange, their visit provides a gracious occasion to publicize your group's activities.

If the powers that be agree to declare the occasion, a student can design and write up a formal proclamation, complete with "Whereas . . .; whereas . . .; therefore we hereby proclaim . . . ." A few students, or the whole group, can bring the proclamation to a meeting of the governmental body to be signed. It makes a nice present for your hosts when you go abroad or your visitors when they arrive.

Letter to the editor

In Brattleboro, Vermont (population about 14,000), many people turn right to the letters to the editor of the newspaper immediately after skimming the front-page headlines. The letters provide a forum where readers respond to the news, vent their anxieties or their spleen, or publicly thank everyone who helped with some community effort. If your local paper's policy welcomes letters to thank the public for its help, write one to thank individuals and organizations who supported your group's activities. Such a letter can't replace individual thank-you notes, but it's a way to acknowledge publicly those people's and groups' generosity.

Making the Best of Bad News

No group of human beings is immune to tragedy, and no amount of planning can avert it. If something terrible happens to anyone in your group—anything from a serious accident to involvement in a crime (either as perpetrator or as victim) to illness or even death—there's little you can do (see "Emergencies," Chapter 12). Publicity will be the last thing you'll be thinking of, so give it a moment's thought before you leave. You'll have all you can do to deal with the situation at hand, so, if possible, arrange to refer all questions to an administrator at school. It will be your job to give him or her the information needed to answer questions from the press.

Be discreet

If you must deal with the press yourself, make sure that your administrators know it. Say as little as you can, for everyone's sake. You might feel better, momentarily, if you share all the details with a sympathetic listener, but that listener shouldn't be a reporter. It wouldn't help the students, their families, your colleagues, or you to see your confidences laid out in cold print the next day. Caution the students to be discreet, too.

Don't be rushed

Take your time, so that you can answer questions as directly as possible, and as briefly. If you don't know the answer to a question, don't fake it; say that you don't know. If you think answering a question would violate someone's privacy, you can say that question isn't for you to answer. The worst that anyone can write is that you refused to comment on a question.

In general, the media are simply trying to inform the public, so there's nothing to fear from them. In fact, when genuine tragedy strikes, you can expect straightforward and considerate treatment. But if reporters see a political slant in an event, or, especially, if they feel that someone is trying to hide something, watch out: they can call you at all hours, dog your footsteps, and ask extremely hostile questions until the controversy finally runs out of steam. Trying to avoid public controversy is more easily said than done, of course, because people can create confrontations about nearly anything.

Don't fight

Faced with a situation that threatens to become political, the best approach is to find all possible points of agreement with the attacker, and to emphasize those. Try to discuss the situation in a cooperative, friendly spirit, assuming that you are both on the same side and interested in achieving the same ends. If that won't work, try to find a way to end the discussion. Don't be drawn into an out-and-out argument, because no one can win. This may seem an odd lesson for a book on student travel, but I learned it the hard way, as the following story may show.

A story

In 1979, when 23 Swiss students visited Brattleboro for the second half of our exchange, the American parents arranged all their sightseeing excursions. An article in the local paper mentioned that the students would visit the Vermont Yankee nuclear power plant.

One Saturday morning at eight o'clock a woman called me. She'd read the newspaper article, and she praised the exchange and the opportunities it offered, but she did have one concern: should the students visit the nuclear plant? Were they, and their parents, aware of possible health risks? Did they know that it was a controversial issue in this area? I tried to reassure her: some of the Swiss students' parents worked for CERN, the European nuclear research center, in Geneva; nuclear power was a controversial issue in Switzerland as well; the visit was optional, so no one who objected would have to go. She thanked me and offered to send me a clipping of the article. I thanked her, and that was that—I thought.

Two days later, the newspaper printed her letter to the editor, voicing exactly the same questions about the scheduled trip, as though we'd never talked at all. I wrote a letter to the editor repeating my reassurance, and that was that—I thought.

The morning of the visit the principal stopped me between classes. "What's this about a demonstration at the power plant?" he asked.

He'd just gotten a call from the assistant superintendent who'd heard on a call-in radio show that some Swiss students were planning to demonstrate against nuclear power during their visit.

My next class waited while I raced to the cafeteria to ask the Swiss students what was going on. Yes, they said, some were planning to wear T-shirts with antinuclear slogans.

Feeling that there was no time to lose (my class was waiting, and the principal would expect answers, right?), I began to argue with the students. I tried to persuade them that a demonstration could hurt the exchange and endanger future exchanges; to emphasize how serious it all was, I told them how the message had come from the administration. They argued that they were expressing their individual feelings, not the group's, and that they would take responsibility for their actions. I countered that they should demonstrate, if they wanted to, on their own time, but not as part of our group. We all got very agitated and didn't resolve anything.

Getting into an argument was the worst way to deal with the situation in the first place. The assistant superintendent had reacted with alarm, the principal had reacted to him, and I'd allowed myself to be drawn into the situation without taking time to think about it. I realized too late that I'd set up a confrontation, a no-win battle of wills; even if the students gave in, we'd be on opposite sides from then on. Too late, I found out that one of the home-stay families had helped the students with their plans; this encouragement weakened my argument that a demonstration would embarrass the families. Too late, I saw that my mention of the administration had impressed them as either a threat (if they didn't cave in, I'd call in the heavy artillery) or martyrdom (the liberal teacher bowing to political pressure).

At noon, the students told me they'd decided to call off the protest. After school we piled into a van and several cars for the trip to the power plant; when we arrived, a tall young man with a portable tape recorder came over to me.

"Mrs. Cassidy?" he said. "I'm Dale Houston of WKVT News. I understand that some Swiss students were planning a silent protest against nuclear power this afternoon, but that school authorities forced them to abandon the idea. Would you care to comment?"

The tape was running. I said that the students had cancelled their plans themselves, but that I had put pressure on them because I didn't want them to offend the Brattleboro families who'd welcomed them.

That night a stringer for the *Rutland Herald* called. Within a day or two, the exchange burst into print in both Rutland and Burlington, at the other end of the state. "T-Shirt 'Censorship' Imbroglio Sours Visit by Swiss Kids," ran one headline. The students had told reporters that they were beginning to wonder whether the U.S. really valued free speech. There wasn't any way to counter these stories without being defensive, so no one at school said anything more; deprived of fuel, the controversy died down.

Be positive

If you get bad press, the issue may not be free speech versus being a good guest. It may be your method of selecting students, or whether the group should miss some school time, or whether certain fund-raising activities are appropriate. Listen carefully if people question your methods, because they are undoubtedly trying to help. Consider each question as a suggestion, and if you can use it, wonderful. If you can't use an idea, don't attack it, putting the questioners on the defensive; instead, explain how you arrived at your way of doing things. They may disagree with you, but there's no harm in that. They will at least appreciate your taking them into your confidence. There's a problem only if they feel defensive or sense defensiveness in you. If you have sound reasons for what you do, if you've tried to communicate those reasons to the students, their parents, the administration, and any other interested party, you've done all you can.

8
Fund Raising

Fund raising is very closely linked with public relations. People are more likely to give money if they know something about your group, and they learn about the group as the students go out into the school or community and explain why they're trying to raise money. Furthermore, once people give money to the group, they have an emotional stake, however small, in the trip's success; they feel involved, and that is one of the purposes of public relations.

Because fund raising depends so heavily on good public relations, perhaps parents and students should discuss the two things together, once the group is formed. You can explain the importance of publicity in winning the public's moral and financial support for the trip. If the group decides to keep accounts of individual students' fund-raising efforts (see "The work bank," later in this chapter), the time they spend on publicity could also go into their "accounts."

Talk it over

Fund raising demands time and energy, so parents and students should talk frankly about their commitment to it. How much time do they want to spend on earning money as a group? Will everyone make an all-out effort, or will several students need to spend a lot of their time earning their own money for the trip—or earning money for college? Your group's fund-raising and public relations campaign will only succeed in raising money, involving the community, and creating *esprit de corps* if it corresponds to the needs of the particular students involved. Before you agree on any specific activities to earn money, the group should discuss and agree on:

- Will everyone be expected to work on fund raising?

- Will parents or other adults in the community also be directly involved?

- Will everyone benefit equally from the group's work, or will the benefits for each student correspond to that student's efforts?

- Will students who drop out of the group be able to recover any of the money they helped the group earn?

- Who will keep track of the money?

- How you will keep track of it (i.e., will you open a bank account? An account with the school's bookkeeper?)

Once the group arrives at the answers to these questions, you can avoid misunderstandings later if you write down the group's decision and have all the students (and perhaps even each student's parent) sign to indicate their understanding and agreement.

As you discuss these questions with the group, you may want to consider three general models for fund raising: the blockbuster, the work bank, and the low-key general effort.

The blockbuster

A unified, all-out fund-raising campaign is wonderful if everyone in the group supports it—or if you're prepared to impose it. When students throw themselves wholeheartedly into earning money for a common goal, the exertion naturally breaks down barriers within the group. You can speed up the process by assigning work teams for various tasks, bringing together students who may think they have nothing in common simply because they don't know each other yet.

The campaign can be the best possible public relations, because the students will be so visible in the community, working hard to earn something worthwhile. Our high school's band set out to raise $30,000 to finance its trip to the Macy's Thanksgiving Day parade in New York. Coordinated by an enthusiastic committee of parents and influential people in the community, the fund raising reached out to everyone in the Brattleboro area. Money just poured in—nearly $40,000 in all. Huge crowds saw the band off on its trip and welcomed it on its return. The band was no longer just the band, it was Our Band, and that extraordinary outpouring of sentiment was intimately related to the community's extraordinary financial contribution to the trip.

This kind of single-minded, all-engrossing effort, so successful when the whole group is behind it, is self-defeating if the students don't support it. It will simply divide the students instead of uniting them: the ones who do less will grumble that they never agreed to get that involved anyway, and the hard workers will resent those who don't pull their weight. Fortunately, fund raising doesn't have to be an all-or-nothing proposition. You still have two alternatives: the work bank and the low-key general effort.

The work bank

The work bank avoids the blockbuster campaign's main problem: there's no pressure on students who really haven't time to devote to raising money with the group. At the same time, students who wish to raise money as a group can do so, secure in the knowledge that their return will be commensurate with the work they put into the fund raising.

Gary Adamski, a French teacher at Montpelier High School, has worked with a group of students to raise several thousand dollars for an exchange with Switzerland. His group set up a work bank, which operates like this: three members of the group keep track of how many hours each student is putting into each fund-raising activity. Thus, every student has an "account," but instead of money, the students "bank" the time they spend baking cookies, soliciting items for a raffle, catering a dinner—in short, doing whatever the group has agreed to do to earn money. Then when it's time to distribute the money in the group's fund, each student's allotment is in proportion to the total amount of time that that student spent working for the group.

"It's so easy!" said Mr. Adamski. "It's in the students' interest to figure out how they're doing, and they all keep a check on each other. They really do it all."

The low-key general effort

I chose this approach for the first two exchanges I organized because I preferred to concentrate my own efforts on orientation activities rather than fund raising. Furthermore, this arrangement encourages responsibility to the group without a lot of pressure.

We didn't set a definite goal for our fund raising. When the group first came together, I distributed an itemized budget for the trip. We agreed that whatever money we earned as a group would simply be deducted from the group's total budget, and the remaining expense would be divided equally among all the students. Therefore it was clear from the outset that everyone would benefit equally from our fund raising, no matter how much or little any one person did. To help the students see the concrete results for their work, I suggested that the money go toward specific budget items (e.g., bus transportation to Boston, health insurance policies). When the group raised more than enough money for those expenses, they decided to save the rest to start a fund to entertain their Swiss counterparts during the second part of the exchange.

Just how low-key your group's fund raising turns out to be will depend on who's involved. One or two volunteers should organize each activity, and if the coordinators are tactful and well-organized, they can mobilize the whole group. Parents, with their energy and their contacts in the community, can give the fund raising a tremendous boost. We raised more money for the Swiss visit here than for our trip abroad, because the parents helped directly with the former effort. They demanded a lot of themselves and of everyone else in the group.

Specific ideas

When your group has agreed on a general approach to fund raising, solicit their ideas for specific ways to raise money. Someone should note all the ideas on a blackboard or large sheet of paper. Encourage the group to consider all the suggestions: no activity is too small if someone is willing to take charge of it, and none is too big if the whole group supports it.

Adding a foreign touch to fund-raising activities will reinforce the group's purpose in the public's mind and will set the group apart from all the other student groups trying to raise money. The following list of fund-raising ideas is only a springboard for your students' ideas. The suggestions are arranged more or less in order according to how much time and effort they require, starting with the more elaborate ideas.

Activity: Sell ads for a program

There may be a great deal of public interest in your group's stay abroad, and there will almost certainly be interest in your visitors' stay in your community. You can print up posters or folding programs listing the main points of either schedule, and then sell advertising space to area businesses or groups. The programs thus raise money for your group, publicize its activities, publicize local attractions that the foreign guests will visit, and recognize the area businesses that help you financially. You may be able to find a printer who'll donate the printing, or at least offer a discount, increasing your profit. If the school has a printshop, ask the printing teacher for help. The group can then ask merchants to display the posters, or students can hand out programs at public events or during bake sales, car washes, etc.

The entire process—pricing the ads, canvassing businesses to sell the advertising space, printing the posters or programs, and then distributing the finished product—demands a high level of knowledge, organization, and commitment. Experience selling ads for a school newspaper or yearbook will help the students who undertake this project. An adult should supervise each fund-raising activity, but ones like this, which are more complex than some of the others and involve business people in the community, require particular attention.

Activity: Ask for direct contributions from businesses and service clubs

Many businesses and organizations set aside money for public relations; some even earmark money specifically to promote education or to help students in some way. The people responsible for allocating such funds are often willing to contribute to a trip. They'll need to understand its educational value, and if they see that students are working hard on their own to pay for the trip, they'll be even more likely to help out.

Parents are often in a better position to appeal to these businesses and groups than are students. Parents know better how to explain the trip's purpose to other adults and they may also know which particular people to approach.

When the group does receive a sizable donation, take a photo of one of the students receiving the check. A photo in the local newspaper or the school newspaper will give publicity both to the group and to whatever organization or business donated the money. (For suggestions about how to take photos for newspapers, see "Photographs," Chapter 7.)

If your group is involved in a two-way exchange, appeals for contributions for the foreign students' visit will probably be more effective than requests for money toward your students' trip abroad. For one thing, the community's pride is involved in showing the visitors a good time; for another, companies can more easily contribute goods and services as well as cash. For example, when the Swiss visited Brattleboro, corporate donations included mountains of pizza and ice cream, oceans of soft drinks, a T-shirt for each visitor, and the use of a van. Of course, such contributions shouldn't be overlooked on a one-way trip, either; if the group itself can't use them or take them to the homestay families as gifts, perhaps it can auction them off or use them as prizes in a raffle. The donor should understand how each donation is to be used: a merchant who donated five gallons of ice cream might be miffed to find it listed as third prize in a raffle if he thought the visitors would enjoy eating it.

Activity: **Organize an auction**

If the group has access to a number of substantial used items, or to new goods or services donated by local businesses, an auction is one way to use them to raise money. The auction can be for the school (e.g., at an assembly) or for the public at large. A school auction can be more informal; a public auction will probably raise more money.

Nearly anything can be auctioned off—to the right buyer. For a school auction, items should obviously appeal to teenagers, who'll bid on free (or heavily discounted) haircuts, records, and posters, as well as gift certificates at stores, restaurants, and movie theaters. Don't forget to solicit items from your colleagues; maybe the horticulture teacher will donate a plant, the industrial-arts teacher a cutting board, the sewing teacher a custom-made skirt or vest. In addition, any teacher may have a contribution that's not related to his or her academic specialty. The principal may have a fantastic recipe for chocolate cake and may be willing to bake one, or any teacher may have some saleable used things in the garage or in the attic.

Of course, students in the group can auction off their services either to the public or to other students. They can offer a catered dinner for six people, or 10 hours of babysitting, or work around the house or yard for a specified amount of time.

For public auctions, the same kinds of things will sell; in addition, adults will bid on antiques, used furniture, and "white elephants"—used household items that can still give use or pleasure to someone. Look over white elephants, and politely decline badly damaged things or small appliances that don't work; they aren't worth the problems they can create.

When soliciting or accepting donations for an auction, make sure the donor understands that you'll sell the donation at whatever price it brings. Donors may want to set a minimum price, or "reserve bid," for their contributions, but bidders will be looking for bargains, and reserve bids would create hard feelings toward your group, the donor, or both; furthermore, you'd have to return items that didn't meet the reserve to their donors.

You'll need an auctioneer. If some of the items are worth $50.00 or more and are likely to attract professional buyers, it might avoid controversy to have a professional or semi-professional auctioneer to auction off at least those valuable items. Talk with auctioneers in your area to negotiate a fee for their services; they might ask for a percentage of the amount they sell rather than a set dollar amount.

For less expensive things, you can line up local celebrities as auctioneers: the mayor, the fire chief, the chairperson of the school committee, the principal, a well-known local sports figure, a disc jockey from a local radio station, and so forth. Such amateurs can add interest and humor to the proceedings, but in fairness to them and to the buyers, they shouldn't have to learn the fundamentals of auctioneering on the job. Arrange for them to meet beforehand to go over the ground rules with someone who can help them.

An auction depends on the bidders who attend. When you schedule it, try to make sure it doesn't conflict with other events in the community. Then—crank out the publicity! Include some of the things to be sold, the name of the professional auctioneer, the names of local celebrities who have agreed to be guest auctioneers, and the fact that the auction will benefit your group.

If the group has access to a local television station, you can run the auction on TV, and bidders can phone in their bids. Gary Adamski's group in Montpelier raised well over a thousand dollars with an auction on local TV. They built up the community's interest in their auction with a gimmick: several pairs of well-known local people (the police chief and the fire chief, the mayor and the losing mayoral candidate) competed to see who was the better auctioneer. It worked like this: each of the rival auctioneers was given a group of nine or ten items to sell. Since both groups had the same estimated total value (say $200.00), whichever of the two people brought in the higher total could claim to be the better auctioneer.

$$\Rightarrow \$-\$\rightarrow$$

Activity: Run a concession at school or community events

A concession—whether at a single event, such as a concert, or at a series of events, such as basketball or football games—can be very profitable. The spectators usually can't go anywhere else for refreshments, and teenagers nearly always seem to be hungry.

Running a concession involves ordering (or making) enough food and drinks, as well as buying cups, napkins, and condiments (hot dogs without mustard, ketchup, and relish will meet with grumbles from the customers); getting plenty of change; arranging for plenty of volunteers to serve the customers, and then cleaning up, disposing of leftover food, and perhaps returning the soft-drink apparatus and collecting the deposit for it.

Before the group commits itself to running a long-term concession, make sure there'll be enough people available to run it *every time*. If the students hedge and say they might have to work, or may have too much studying or may be going away, it's better not to get involved, since both the events' sponsor and the spectators have a right to expect consistency.

If the students do make the effort, a successful concession, like most fund raising, can help the public learn about the group. The students can put up posters with the group's logo or the flag of the country they'll be visiting; they can distribute explanatory leaflets or programs; and they should be prepared to talk about the exchange or trip with people who express an interest in it.

$$\Rightarrow \$-\$\rightarrow$$

Activity: Cater a foreign dinner

Serving foreign dinners is another of Gary Adamski's successes.

"Everybody likes to eat out," he said, "and you can't beat the quality or the price of our dinners." His group buys ingredients in bulk, works together to make and serve the food, and makes several hundred dollars' profit from each dinner.

Effective publicity will draw diners to your table. Emphasize the menu's variety and abundance, and use posters and free "community calendars"—announcements in newspapers or on the radio—to spread the word.

The group might want to offer entertainment after dinner. They could show slides of past trips, or sing songs in another language, or perform brief skits. The entertainment should please the general public, from grandparents to toddlers, so keep it informal—and short.

Activity: **Ask a local business to donate part of a day's receipts**

A merchant or restaurant owner may be willing to declare a certain day "Send the Students Day," or "German Exchange Day"; your group would receive a small percentage of that day's receipts. Perhaps the business prefers to donate only when customers indicate that they're aware of the donation and support it. Customers can show their support in a variety of ways: simply by mentioning Send the Students Day, by presenting a ticket or leaflet your students have distributed, by giving their sales slips to students in the group, or by leaving sales slips in a specially-marked depository right in the store.

The students should have plenty of time to publicize Send the Students Day, to generate income and goodwill for both the group and its benefactor. They can use posters, announcements at school and in the media, and word of mouth.

Activity: **Work days**

The group can spend a Saturday doing odd jobs. They can rake leaves, clean house, shovel snow, weed a garden, paint a garage, or do anything else that needs stamina and enthusiasm rather than particular skills; they can babysit.

The group should set some ground rules:

- How much will they charge per hour?

- Who's responsible for transportation?

- Is it preferable to work in teams of two or three students? It might be safer, it's probably just as efficient, and it's certainly more fun than working alone.

- How can potential employers get in touch with workers? It's helpful to have a phone number that people can call for several days before the work day; perhaps a family would volunteer its phone if using the school's phone is impractical.

- How will you publicize the work day? Posters in supermarkets and laundromats can supplement radio and newspaper announcements and word of mouth communication among the students' neighbors and the faculty.

You (or whoever supervises the activity) should help the students gracefully decline work that could harm them in some way. One hot day I was part of a student work crew hired at nominal rates to clear dead plants from a householder's ditch. Later we all broke out in allergic reactions, and discovered that we'd been clearing dead but still active poison ivy. The money we'd earned was hardly worth the itching (to say nothing of the cortisone shots required to control the allergy). As we were graduate students, we had only our own ignorance to blame, but high school students could benefit from adult guidance.

Activity: **Hold a raffle**

The group can raffle off anything, from just one prize to a large number of donated goods and services. Our group raised over $125 when we raffled off a single five-pound chocolate bar, which we'd displayed in all its rich, chocolaty glory in a showcase at school. When the group asks merchants and other businesses to donate prizes for the raffle, it would be tactful not to approach the same ones who have already donated something for an auction; there's no use taxing the goodwill of the very people who have helped the most.

A NOTE ABOUT RAFFLE TICKETS: be sure to number them and record the numbers of the tickets each student is given to sell. Each buyer should write a phone number or homeroom number on every ticket, so the group can get in touch with the winners.

Activity: **Sell candy, Christmas cards, light bulbs, etc.**

A sure way to make money is to sell some of the merchandise offered by the companies that specialize in sales through school groups. Though the companies compete aggressively to win students' orders, selling arrangements (as well as the quality of the merchandise) vary from one company to the next, so be sure that the group knows what it's getting and what its obligations are. The group shouldn't buy the merchandise outright before taking orders; customers can pay when they order, or else the group should be able to return any unsold merchandise.

What sells? People will buy anything that's moderately priced, if the students are selling it with enthusiasm. Practical items aren't necessarily the most saleable; often people already have the things they really need, and they're glad to buy things they don't need at all —"to help out the kids." If you need ideas and you're not on any companies' mailing lists, ask around among your colleagues who are club advisers; they'll probably have more brochures than they can use.

Some ideas:

- school-spirit items (pencils, buttons, bumper stickers, caps, even blazers, warm-up suits, and windbreakers in school colors with the school's emblem);
- stationery and gift wrapping;
- candy (though some schools restrict the sale of candy in the school itself);
- inexpensive jewelry;
- candles;
- T-shirts: companies have T-shirts for every taste, appealing to everyone from monster movie fans to motorcycle freaks;
- beach towels;
- lightbulbs;
- linen dish towels, sometimes with a calendar printed on them;

- photographic portraits;
- inexpensive crystal (glasses and serving pieces).

Activity: Sponsor a benefit dance or a variety show

A variety show requires little financial risk but enormous organization and plenty of time; a dance is easier to organize but may require an investment to pay for the band or disc jockey (and perhaps a hall or police deputies). Still, both activities can raise a lot of money in a community accustomed to such events, provided that they're carefully scheduled and organized. Either of these activities will bring in even more money if it's combined with a concession or even a catered dinner.

Activity: Put canisters near merchants' cash registers

Retail business people and restaurant owners may be willing to give counter space to canisters into which people can drop contributions as they receive their change. The students can make canisters from empty coffee cans by painting them or wrapping them in paper and cutting slits in their plastic tops.

This approach demands even more public understanding of the trip than other approaches. There's no face-to-face communication between a potential contributor and the students in the group, and so there is no chance for the students to explain the trip and their involvement in it. It helps if the canisters themselves show the group's name, its logo if it has one, and some information about the trip to help people understand where their money is going.

The business people themselves can in a sense represent the group to the public, if they thoroughly understand and support the trip. It pays to take the time to talk with them or to give them an informational leaflet so they'll be able to inform their customers about the trip's value for the students.

Activity: Deliver messages or flowers at school

A message service can be organized in school at any time, but it's especially appropriate just before Christmas, Valentine's Day, or a big dance. Anyone who wants to send a message (possibly anonymous) to someone in school can pay a small fee to a member of the group, who will then deliver the message to the addressee's homeroom. The group can advertise this service ahead of time in posters and announcements, take in messages (and money) for two or three days in a some central spot in school, and then deliver all the messages on a given day.

This service is pure profit; the group may also want to elaborate on it by delivering a flower with each message. A florist might be willing to give the group a substantial discount on the flowers (thus increasing the profit on them), especially for a large order; ask. (The florist would need advance notice anyway, to be sure of having enough flowers of a particular kind or color on hand.) The group runs no financial risk in this venture, since the fee accompanies each advance order. The service is even more appealing when the sender can specify the color of the flowers; colored roses are especially suitable. Red roses mean love, yellow ones symbolize friendship, and so forth.

Activity: Sell bumper stickers or buttons

I've made a separate category for selling buttons and bumper stickers because they're so inexpensive and easy to obtain that they usually don't require complicated arrangements with a large company as other things do. Still, even though they don't cost the group much, they can't command a very high price, so the only way to make up for the small profit margin is to sell huge numbers of them.

Of course you can print anything—from the school emblem to funny sayings to your group's logo—on the stickers or buttons. When the group is deciding what to print, consider that these items can build public involvement and support as well as earn money. When people wear buttons saying, "I support the Spanish Club Trip," or display bumper stickers saying, "Learning Is a Foreign Affair: Centerville High School-Mexico Exchange," they're spreading the word to others who don't yet know anything about the trip. Of course, in order to buy these items advertising the trip, people will already have to know about it, support it, and feel involved in it. Once again, understanding builds support, which encourages contributions, which increases interest, which leads to further understanding, in a cycle of growing public involvement with the group.

Activity: Wash cars

A car wash is a simple way to earn money without committing too much of the group's time or money. A successful car wash requires:

- a location where there's lots of local traffic moving slowly enough so that drivers can stop conveniently;
- an adequate water supply: perhaps the fire company will allow the group to use a hydrant, or a parent will donate water, even if it's metered;
- hoses, buckets, sponges, detergent. If the group plans to clean cars' interiors, it will also need a vacuum cleaner (CAUTION: Students should use any electrical appliances *far away* from the washing area, to avoid the risk of electrical shock);
- posters to attract drivers' notice to the car wash;
- advance publicity: newspaper and radio announcements, posters in supermarkets and laundromats;
- a cashbox with change;
- an enthusiastic crew of students;
- good weather (good luck!).

Activity: Collect paper, cans or bottles for recycling

One person's trash is another person's trip abroad. Is there a buyer in your area for glass bottles, aluminum cans, or old newspapers? If so, the group can earn a respectable amount of money collecting the stuff and delivering it to the buyer. The collection can be random, with the group simply going from door to door on the spur of the moment, or it can be highly organized, with advance publicity to allow families to store up the material and a telephone number for them to call for pickup on an appointed day.

Activity: Hold a tag sale or bake sale

A tag sale requires some organization, but almost no investment; a bake sale demands a small investment and some time to do the baking (though if the group buys ingredients in bulk and bakes together—e.g., in the home economics kitchen at school—the baking will be less costly and more fun).

A tag sale can take place in front of someone's house or in a flea market booth. Though bake sales can also be successful at flea markets, they'll do well anywhere there's a lot of foot traffic: at school, or in front of a bank or supermarket, or at a busy shopping center. The group may need to ask permission to sell at those places.

Price to sell! People will be happy to get bargains, and merchandise that stays on the table doesn't earn anything. Besides, you'll have to dispose of it later.

Don't forget to identify the group through posters or leaflets. People like to know whom they're helping.

Activity: Combine these ideas

Sell baked goods at a car wash; sell raffle tickets or bumper stickers while going from house to house for a bottle drive, or during a catered dinner. Of course the group won't want to overwhelm people, or beg for money all the time—but if the students are polite, enthusiastic about what they're doing, and appreciative, their efforts will seem not obnoxious, but enterprising. People, like God, prefer to help those who help themselves.

9

Get Ready—
Orientation

Why is orientation necessary?

The scene is a sit-down dinner, the culminating orientation activity for the Swiss exchange. The American students are in someone's home eating unfamiliar foods—speaking French the entire time. Val takes one look at her first course, a bowl of cream soup, and announces, in pidgin French, "I can't eat this. I will throw up." Other students in the group laugh nervously.

Val's response to the stress of a new situation isn't unusual among American teenagers: not knowing how to react, they often overreact on purpose. Another common response is to cling desperately to the familiar: for example, many students simply hope that everyone they meet will speak English. In order to break free from these natural but unfortunate patterns, students need to go through an orientation program before they travel abroad. Just as athletes need to train and actors need to rehearse, student travelers need a chance to practice new linguistic and cultural situations before they face the real pressure of communicating with native speakers far from home.

Orientations sessions are different from informational meetings: in orientation, students actually role-play situations they're almost certain to meet during their trip. Orientation makes students take the crucial first steps into the other culture: they realize that it's up to them to behave appropriately, and with help from you and each other they have a chance to learn how to do that without the risk of offending anyone. In these practice situations they can afford to step back and look at their own reactions and other students', talk about why those reactions were or weren't appropriate, and share ideas about how to deal with their nervousness in positive ways. In Val's case, for example, other students probably laughed because they too were wondering whether they could eat the food, what would happen if they refused, and what would happen if they couldn't figure out how to refuse. At the time, I politely ignored Val's *gaffe*, but after the dinner the group talked about their homestay families' expectations, some foods they might encounter, and how to express their preferences in acceptable ways.

Thus, orientation gives the students a chance to fail without grave consequences: they can learn from their mistakes and correct them. When they are abroad, they can approach a situation with confidence: they have an idea of what to expect and what's expected of them, and they know they can get through it successfully: they've already done that in orientation.

Besides the students' increased confidence and competence, orientation has other benefits: it allows you to get to know your group in the context of travel. Sometimes students who are weak in class are the most resourceful when they're away from home. At the same time, of course, the members of the group are getting to know themselves and each other; they are often surprised to learn who knows a lot about your destination, who can communicate easily, and who is a natural leader.

Keep in mind . . .

During orientations, as during the trip as a whole, the teacher functions as a coach. There are always a couple of clowns who cover their nervousness by pretending to rob the bank instead of changing their money, and I try to maintain the character of the bank-teller—but then I insist that they go through the role-play again as American teenagers instead of bandits. Some students can't get through a situation the first time; we talk about how to approach the problem, and then, if it's practical, I encourage them to try it again right away. In this way they won't be left thinking, "I can't do this." Furthermore, other students will also understand that even though all the participants have different personalities and levels of competence in the target language, all of them can—and must—learn to behave appropriately, to make the trip more pleasant for everyone.

It's important to find a balance between realism and make-believe in orientation activities. Each situation should be realistic enough to challenge the students, and yet clearly make-believe, so that they can feel free to try out reactions they might not dare to try in a real situation. It's also important to establish a positive, supportive atmosphere, so they will understand that they can falter, or blunder, and no one will mind. You can set the tone by making sure that everyone does all the exercises, and by including everyone in discussion. That way they can all learn from each other; no one feels superior, no one feels picked on, and no one feels left out.

Discussion after each orientation activity is essential to give the students a chance to talk over their feelings and put them in perspective. At times students will be eager to talk; sometimes they'll be reluctant; in either case, allow time for discussion, and encourage them to air their reactions and ask questions.

Jenny Brown, a colleague who has led trips to France, Spain, and Mexico, emphasizes how much students learn from each other during orientation.

"Orientation is a chance for kids to learn not only how to be a guest in another country—for some it's a chance to learn how to be a guest, period," she says. "The trick is to get kids who do know to articulate what they know so that kids who don't know yet can learn without having to admit they don't know."

Since orientation is so important to making the trip successful for everyone, we make it clear at the outset of our travel programs that attendance at orientation is mandatory. Since this kind of travel is probably new to students, they may not see how important their preparation is. After a few sessions they will probably begin to understand its usefulness.

If any students missed more than one or two sessions, I would first warn them; then, if they continued to miss meetings, I would not allow them to go on the trip. A group of travelers is only as strong as its weakest members, and students who don't invest the time to prepare well for the experience shouldn't be allowed to spoil it for those who do. Whether their poor attendance was due to forgetfulness, illness, lack of motivation, arrogance, or simply the inability to organize their time—they would be unprepared for the trip, and would demand too much time and attention from you and everyone else. It wouldn't be fair to anyone, particularly their homestay families.

Of course no amount of orientation can completely prepare your students for what they'll experience. Although you understand this, your students may not, and they may blame you later, saying, "But you told us. . . !" They'll understand eventually; it may help if you explain at the beginning that its purpose is to help them develop *both the skills and the attitude they'll need in order to meet new situations.* No specific vocabulary-list or role-play will be as useful to them as flexibility and a sense of humor as they meet whatever comes their way. Ideally, orientation should help students cultivate both these qualities in themselves.

Plan orientation sessions

Here are two sample orientation schedules: one includes eighteen sessions, the other eleven.

Note: RP - role play

ORIENTATION SCHEDULE: EIGHTEEN SESSIONS

1. Nonverbal paired interview or dialogue (RP); topics for finding out about host country
2. Individual interviews; pretest
3. Presentation of some reports on host country; going through customs (RP); instructions for getting passports
4. Presentation of some reports; basic polite expressions
5. My town/your town (RP); towns and cities
6. Currency (denominations, exchange rates); the bank (RP)
7. Metrics; problem list (RP)
8. Family photos; check passports
9. American as others see us (RP); talk about projects
10. Parts of the body; illness; using the phone (RP)
11. Houses; in a new family
12. Public transport; shopping
13. Table-setting vocabulary; food
14. Orientation dinner; present projects

See Chapter 10, "Get Set—" for the following topics:

15. Journals; presents for homestay families; present more projects
16. Packing; electricity/media; security
17. Luggage hike
18. Meet with families: itinerary, phone tree, rules of conduct, emergencies, culture shock, health

ORIENTATION SCHEDULE: ELEVEN SESSIONS

Most topics are detailed in this chapter; the rest are from Chapter 10, "Get Set—".

1. General knowledge of the country
2. Courtesy, greetings, thank-you's; talking about why you are in the host country (RP)
3. Bathroom, getting lost, saying you're sorry (RP)
4. Food, table manners
5. Shopping, money, checks (RP)
6. Packing, gift for host family; checking passports; arranging transportation to airport
7. Art/history
8. Mail, telephone (RP), electricity/media
9. Field-trip permission forms, catching up with details
10. Culture shock, health (RP), security
11. Luggage hike; farewell meeting with families: itinerary, phone tree, rules of conduct, emergencies.

All this orientation means enormous amount of work for everyone—for the students, and, especially, for you. I don't think of it as "extra" work because for me it is part of the whole experience, not merely preparation for it, but it's certainly a lot of work, no matter how you think of it. Is it really worth it? Yes, but you may have to see it to believe it. One of the first and most important discoveries that students make when they travel is that *not* everybody speaks English; orientation equips them to handle that discovery and use it to build their own communication skills. You'll know it was worthwhile when a student rushes up to you and says, "I did it! I cashed my check just like we did in orientation, and it's a good thing I could, because I could speak more French than that teller did English!"

Note: I've written up all the following activities as though you, the trip's leader, would be directing them. If you aren't comfortable in the target language, but wish to work on it with your students, a language teacher or an advanced student may take charge of the language activities. "You" refers to whoever is directing each activity.

Help students find out about the host country

Knowing something about the place they'll be visiting not only will make that place more real to your students, but also will endear them to their hosts.

One way to encourage students to find out about where they're going is to ask individuals or small groups to report on various topics to the rest of the group. The reports give the students useful practice in research techniques, even though the end product may be a very informal oral report.

To help the students come up with topics for these reports, give each one a blank piece of paper, and ask them all to draw a vertical line down the middle of the sheet. On the left they should write what comes to mind when they hear the country's name; what do they already know about the country? On the right-hand side they should list things they'd like to know more about concerning the new country. When they've all finished, ask each student to tell the group one thing he wrote, and write all the ideas on a big sheet of paper or the blackboard to make a group list. Discuss each item as it comes up, if that seems appropriate. They can then choose the topics for their reports from the list of things they'd like to know more about. If there aren't enough ideas to go around, some suggestions follow:

- history (perhaps divided into various time-periods or subtopics)

- governmental structure

- famous citizens of the country

- the national anthem or hymn (so the students will at least recognize it when they hear it)

- tourist attractions

- the country's currency

- major industries

- geography (important cities, rivers, mountain ranges)

- current problems and issues (political, social, economic)

- food

Another possibility is to set up an area somewhere in the school (e.g., in a corner of a classroom or in the library) to display materials about the host country. Encourage the students to bring in postcards, maps, newspaper clippings, posters, magazine articles, souvenirs, advertising—anything connected with the other country. Ask one of the students to be in charge of this area; she can keep track of who has brought in what. Encourage all the students to keep abreast of what's there; point out specific things you find interesting or useful.

Finally, don't overlook human resources. Are there people in the school or in the community who have traveled to your host country? Even if their experiences were quite different from what your students' will probably be, the group may find them very interesting, and they may have some useful insights and suggestions for your students.

***Activity:* Nonverbal paired interview**

This exercise works best for groups of people who don't already know each other; groups who do should use the nonverbal dialogue (below).

Arrange pairs of students who don't know each other; if they don't know each other's names, introduce them. Explain that they have five minutes to find out all they can about their partners *in any way that doesn't use words.* They may draw pictures or use gestures, but they may neither speak nor write any words. After five minutes, give them a signal to switch partners. When the time's up, form a circle; each person reports to the group on what he's learned about his partner. In this way, everyone in the group learns something about each person.

Discussion: What gestures did they understand easily? Which ones gave them trouble? Were they frustrated? Was it fun? Was this a useful exercise? Why or why not?

Activity: **Nonverbal dialogue**

For students who already know each other well, a paired interview would be artificial. Pair up students who do know each other, and tell them that they'll have five minutes to make arrangements to go out together—*without using words.* Where will they go? What time? How will they get there? Where will they meet? When the five minutes are up, one person from each pair can tell the whole group the details of that pair's arrangement.

Discussion: the same as in the paired interview (above).

Activity: **Taking directions**

Everyone should have paper and a pencil. One person draws a geometric figure (for example: ⌂▭○) and doesn't show it to anyone. Then that person gives directions to the others so they can draw the same figure. He or she may not look at the others' papers, and they may not speak at all, either to ask questions or to comment on what's going on. When the direction-giver is finished, all compare their drawings with the original.

Then another person (perhaps the person who most nearly imitated the first drawing) can make a drawing and give instructions to others. This time they may ask questions, but *only questions that can be answered by yes or no.*

Discussion: Which procedure produced the best drawings? Which was more pleasant for the person giving instructions? For the people trying to follow directions? Why? Is this game like going to another country? How? Is it a useful exercise? Why or why not?

Activity: **My town/your town**

This exercise is meant both for groups who are involved in two-way exchanges, and for groups who are simply going to a homestay. Ask the latter to imagine that they'll be hosting a group, just for this exercise.

Without consulting each other, students should make two lists: one of things they want to be sure to see while they're abroad, and the other of things that they'd like their visitors to see during their visit to the U.S.

When they've finished, form a circle. Each person should read one item from his or her first list, giving reasons for wanting to see that particular thing. Then, again by turns around the circle, students should read the items from their second list, explaining why they'd like visitors to see each thing.

Discussion: Were all the first lists similar? All the second lists? Why or why not? Were the first lists similar to the second lists? If not, how did they differ? Who should determine what visitors see—the hosts or the visitors themselves?

Activity: **Americans as others see us**

I adapted this exercise from a Center for Latin American Studies curriculum report called "Cross—Cultural Inquiry; Value Clarification Exercises." The report, by J. Doyle Casteel, Clemens Hallman and others, is available of microfiche through the ERIC system (ask for it at your library). It has many useful activities for students going to Latin America, but I found this exercise useful for *anyone* about to travel abroad for the first time; people don't realize that, in the eyes of host nationals they meet, they represent the United States.

At first my students reacted with outrage: 'I don't know anything about any of this stuff! I'm just a kid." We talked about the questions, partial answers for some of them, and ways to deal with this sort of question without going on the defensive or putting the questioner on the defensive. Of course they did often encounter questions like this in Switzerland, though the tone of the questions was much friendlier.

Americans as others see us

You are the editor of a respected American newspaper, and you're the guest speaker at a conference of journalists from all over the world. You've agreed to answer questions submitted by the journalists about your country. When you get the list of questions, you're struck by their tone; you're further struck by the accompanying note, which says that because of a change in schedule you'll only have time to answer three questions.

Choose the three questions you will answer, without discussing your choices.

1. Why do you have so much poverty and unemployment when your country is so rich and technologically advanced?

2. Why do American women work outside the home, thus increasing divorce, juvenile delinquency, and unemployment for men who need to support their families?

3. Is it true that youth go to school and yet can't read, and that they use drugs and alcohol in school?

4. Why does your country, which has democratic tradition, support dictatorships in Latin America?

5. Why do Americans know so little about the rest of the world, and why don't they learn other languages?

6. Why does your government allow your businessmen to get rich on other countries' resources and sell their expensive goods in underdeveloped countries, instead of helping the countries, develop their own industries for their own needs?

7. How is it that a film star can be president of your country? Why is there no control over who is chosen, or why did you choose him, when the safety and future of the whole world depend on that one person?

8. Why does your country spend so much money on arms when there are people sleeping in your streets?

Discussion: How did you feel when you read the list of questions? Which three questions did you choose to answer? Why? How would you answer the questions you chose? Where might these images of the U.S. have come from?

Do you have any similar questions in the back of your mind about the country you'll be visiting? How can you formulate the questions to get answers without offending your hosts?

Activity: **Polite expressions**

Even if students don't speak a word of the host country's language when they sign up for the trip, and even if they won't be staying with families, a very few expressions in the foreign language are essential to smooth their communication with people they meet. If you don't know these phrases yourself, find someone who can teach them to you and the group.

The essential expressions:

- Good day.
- Goodbye.
- Excuse me (as an introduction or interruption rather than as an apology): Excuse me, where is . . .?
- I'm sorry (as when you step on someone's foot).
- I speak English.
- I am an American student.
- Please.
- Thank you.
- You're welcome.
- Yes.
- No.
- Where is this? (pointing to a name or a map)
- Numbers—counting from one to several hundred, if possible.

With this very basic vocabulary, it's possible to communicate quite a lot—simply, but politely: "Excuse me, please. Where is this?" (Pointing to a map, or the name of a place.) "I'm sorry, I speak English . . . Thank you very much. Goodbye." Of course this vocabulary doesn't help students understand people they meet, but it will allow them to make contact with people in the most positive and polite way; when that first encounter is pleasant, they'll be amazed to see how much they can express and understand through gestures and smiles. They'll also be amazed at the efforts people will make to help them.

Activity: **Houses**

Rural and suburban students are sometimes surprised that even in well-off Western European countries, many middle-class families live in apartments, not houses at all.

A useful vocabulary-building exercise and kickoff for discussion is to make a list of the components of a house: ask the students for the English names of the rooms, pieces of furniture, appliances. Then list (in the host language) all the components of a house where they're going. Be sure to tell them about things or ways of arranging them that aren't common in the American culture (e.g., the *bidet;* the fact that doors may have handles, not knobs, or that the toilet may not be in the bathroom, but off by itself); the students will feel more relaxed and at home if they know what to expect from their new surroundings.

This list can be the basis for discussion not only of the new physical environment, but also of the new way of life as it's reflected in that environment. For example, the French have small refrigerators because they shop every day, not once a week; so many Europeans live in apartments because Europe is small and densely populated compared to the U.S., and land is getting too expensive for middle-class families to afford.

Activity: Towns and cities

This exercise is similar to "Houses." By looking at the layout of a typical town in the host country, the students get a chance to become familiar with vocabulary before they're actually walking down the street. Some cultural differences can emerge in a relatively painless way, too: knowing that there's a horse butcher helps prepare one for the possibility of eating horse meat.

Activity: Going through customs

Although many countries require only that tourists show their passports to an official, "Customs" can be a useful role-play.

Give each student a "passport": a folded piece of construction paper about the size of an American passport will do fine. If they'll be arriving at their destination by air, ask them to line up with their imaginary luggage. If they'll be crossing the border by train or bus, arrange chairs appropriately. Then you take the role of the customs or immigration officer. Ask them all for their passports; ask them to indicate their luggage, and ask one or two to open theirs. Ask a few how long they'll be staying, in what hotel they're staying, where they're from, whether a teacher is with them, and so on—all in very official tones. If someone reacts inappropriately, feign bafflement or embarrassment, and ask others in the group to interpret that person's words or intent.

Discussion: explain that though they almost certainly won't get so much attention from customs officials, they will be asked some of those questions constantly, so they should prepare answers. Ask what additional vocabulary they need in order to feel comfortable with these questions.

Activity: The bank

Simulating a transaction at a bank is doubly useful because students can practice basic polite expressions as they learn about the new system of money and how to use it.

First of all, the currency itself may communicate a lot about the history or culture of the host country. Why is the unit of curreny called a *franc* or a *bolivar*? What historical personages are pictured on the coins or bills? What is their importance to the host country? Pass around some coins or bills so that students can look at them closely.

Some students have a hard time understanding that a dollar may be worth 7.12 French francs today and 6.82 French francs next month. To show them how currency values fluctuate daily, you can distribute copies of the international currency exchange, printed daily in major newspapers. I also draw a facsimile exchange chart like the ones they'll see in the banks where they change their money; then I explain the columns that are labeled "sale" and "purchase," so they'll see that when they're exchanging their dollars for foreign currency the bank is really buying those dollars. Even if they don't grasp the principle very firmly, at least they'll know where to look for the appropriate exchange rate when they're changing their money.

Use a ditto master to print up facsimile traveler's checks in various denominations, and distribute a few to each student. Explain to the group (or have a student explain) how to use the checks. Then set up a facsimile bank, perhaps with separate places for a teller and cashier, and have the students bring their checks for "cashing." Depending on their level, you can prepare them (rehearsing a dialogue, for example, or giving them a sheet with essential phrases on it) — or they can plunge in with no preparation. In any case, you and a colleague or advanced students can play the bank employees: pretend to understand no English at all; ask for their passports; insist that they sign the checks in front of you; use typical phrases, and, in general, act like a non-English-speaking bank employee in the host country. If someone is completely at a loss, suggest (in your role as bank teller) that other students help out. Make a show of counting out imaginary money, asking them if they want large bills or change. I generally set the exchange rate very precisely so they don't expect round numbers, and so they'll get practice hearing change counted out to them.

Students usually enjoy this activity, and its usefulness is obvious, so they don't mind repeating it. If they need a phrase sheet the first time around, I ask them to go through it again without one. By this time they've seen and heard so many other students that they generally have no trouble on their own, and their confidence soars.

Discussion: What phrases did they hear? What polite expressions did they use? Did anything surprise them? Was the activity useful? Why or why not? (When students articulate for themselves what they have learned, the telling of it seems to reinforce the learning.)

Activity: The post office

This is essentially the same exercise as at the bank, except that students will probably need some specialized vocabulary, so that they can ask for aerograms, or for their packages to be weighed, insured, sent surface mail or airmail, etc. Many large post offices have different windows for different purposes, so they'll need to know some vocabulary even to find the right place to transact their business.

Stamps are often beautiful and can show even more about the country than its currency does: stamps can depict animals, plants, natural wonders, sports events, monuments and buildings—nearly anything that is important to the host culture. Suggest that students look for especially attractive or interesting stamps; they make inexpensive and easily stored souvenirs.

Activity: Using the phone

Students generally welcome a chance to practice using the phone before they get into a situation where they *must* use it.

You may need to introduce vocabulary or even explain how a pay phone works if it's very different from an American phone. Then hand out cards at random. On each card will be instructions to make a specific call. Either you or some students who are comfortable speaking the foreign language can play the people on the other end of the line; these people should not only give the requested information, but also present questions and choices: "In whose name is that reservation? . . . Could you please spell that?" "Do you want to leave in the morning or the afternoon?"

Some suggestions for calls:

- Call your homestay family to say you missed the bus and will be late for dinner.

- Call the station to get departure times and ticket prices for a train to Madrid.

- Make reservations for dinner at a restaurant.

- Call a cinema to ask what film is playing and what time it starts.

- Call a friend who's not home; leave a message for her to call back.

- Reserve seats at a theater (the theater can offer seats at various prices).

- Call a new acquaintance and invite him or her to the movies with you and your homestay brother or sister.

- Call the library to ask what its hours are.

- Make an appointment with a doctor (and explain what's wrong).

- Call for a taxi (giving the time it's needed and your address).

- Call the airport to find out when the morning flight from Rome arrives.

Discussion: What phrases did you use or hear?

Activity: **Public transit**

Some of my students had never taken a subway. Since I knew we'd be taking one to get from the airport to our hotel in Paris, I devoted one orientation session to the Paris *métro* system, and what route we'd take to the hotel. It turned out that we arrived at a different airport from the one I'd shown them—but at least they had an idea how to use the system. If you won't be using public transportation right away, or if you yourself aren't very familiar with it, this orientation can wait until you arrive at your destination.

Try to obtain copies of a public transit map of the city (write to the host country's embassy, consulate, or tourist bureau in the U.S.). First explain the system in general; about how much it costs, when and where to pay and any other relevant details (e.g., in many countries certain seats are reserved for the elderly, the handicapped, and pregnant women; in Geneva, bus passengers pay on the honor system—and if the occasional *contrôleur* catches you not paying, watch out!). Then set problems: for each one, find a central location, and ask students how to go from there to another specific location via public transportation.

Activity: **Metrics**

On the whole, American students are much more familiar with the metric system than they used to be, but for many of them metrics are still confined to the math classroom and the science lab; few know their own weight in kilos or their height in meters. You may want to spend at least part of an orientation session helping them brush up on their metric conversion.

After presenting the essential information, which can be found in almost any dictionary if the students don't know it by heart, you can ask them to figure out the answers to the following commonly asked questions:

- their weight in kilos

- their height in meters

- the distance in kilometers between their houses and the school

- how many liters of gasoline their family car holds, and how many kilometers it gets to the liter of gas

- how much gasoline costs per liter at home

- the distance in kilometers between their town and a large city

Activity: **Problem list**

This is purely a springboard for discussion. Each problem is based not on American students' rudeness or thoughtlessness (as one might think at first glance), but on differences between American and French cultures or the special relationship between a student and a host family. You can adapt the list to reflect the particular culture that your group will be encountering.

Distribute copies of the list; if your students can handle it, translate it into the host language. Explain that these are problems homestay families have had with their American guests, and ask the students to rank the problems, putting a "1" next to the one they think is most serious, a "2" by the next-most-important one, and so on. They should not discuss the list at first. When all the students, working alone, have put the problems in order, they should form small groups and try to come up with a consensus within each group as to which problems are the most important; then the whole group can discuss each item on the list.

  a. He stays in bed after the rest of the family is awake and up.

  b. She's not interested in our rich culture and history.

  c. He uses the telephone just to talk with his friends.

  d. She doesn't tell us when she'll be home.

  e. He wastes food.

  f. She sits in her room and writes letters all day.

  g. He stays in the bathroom too long.

  h. He helps himself to food from the refrigerator.

Discussion: What could be the cause of each of these problems? What can a student do to avoid them?

The following brief explanations of the origin of each problem may contribute to the group's discussion.

    a. The family feels responsible for giving the student breakfast and getting his day organized. They need to know when he'll be home, whether he'll need a key, whether he needs lunch, and so on. Besides, if he's sleeping they won't want to wake him up, and will feel especially constrained not to make noise.

    b. It's up to the student to show interest—by spending time with the family even when they're not doing anything in particular, by taking an interest in everything, and by asking questions to satisfy that interest. Students often wait to be shown or told things, but host families usually don't take the lead in pointing things out to their guests, for fear of boring them. When their guests express curiosity, though, most families will go to great lengths to satisfy it.

c. In many countries the telephone is not as universally available as it is in the U.S., and it's much more expensive. American students may not realize how expensive their casual calls are for the host families. Offering to pay won't always solve the problem; in many cultures people simply don't use the phone unless they need to.

d. Because the American students are so far away from home, the host families sometimes feel even more direct responsibility for them than the students' own parents do; the host families can't take the students' well-being for granted, as their American parents naturally do. The family will plan meals around their guest, wait up for her, and worry if she doesn't come back exactly when she's supposed to. They ask themselves, "What could we tell her parents if something happened to her?" The American students have to take this well-meant concern into account, though at times it may irritate or inconvenience them.

e. French families found this the most serious problem of all. French families, on the average, spend nearly 25% of their income on food. They also devote a lot of attention to it, and they're proud of their food. If their guests says casually, "Oh, I'm not hungry—I just had a hamburger in town," the family will feel insulted and upset.

f. A host family may feel rejected if their student closets herself in her room rather than spending time with them—even if they're not actually doing something special. They're afraid she's miserable, that she doesn't like them, that she's writing to her American family to tell them how unhappy she is. It's natural for students to want to write to their family and friends, but they should take care not to seem to withdraw from their host families.

g. Americans tend to take endless supplies of hot water for granted, while in other countries it's often much more expensive or limited in quantity, or both. Another problem is that while many American houses and apartments have two or more bathrooms, in other countries the whole family may share one bathroom. Scheduling may be tight, especially at certain times of the day.

h. Though now, as fast food threatens to take over the world, eating patterns are beginning to change in many places, Americans are still more addicted to nibbling between meals than many nationalities. American refrigerators are enormous, and Americans buy food for several days at a time. Host families who have just enough food for today's lunch and dinner will be dismayed to see that their guest has eaten part of it for a between-meal snack.

Activity: **Family photos**

The students' homestay families will be very interested in snapshots of their American families. Ask the students to bring photos of their families to an orientation session. Pair the students so that they don't know their partners very well. Each student should then show his photos and describe his family in the host language, and his partner will play the role of someone in the homestay family. Encourage the "hosts" to ask questions about the "guests'" house, lifestyle, etc., as well as factual questions about the American families. Then the partners switch roles.

Discussion: What was easy to describe? What seemed hard? What vocabulary words would make it easier next time? Was this activity worthwhile? Why or why not?

Activity: Electricity/audio

Students who intend to take electrical appliances with them will have to invest in converters and/or plug adapters. This will be a particular concern to the wearers of soft contact lenses, who need to boil the lenses. If the adaptive equipment seems too cumbersome or too expensive, they can plan to boil their lenses on their homestay families' stoves (if your city-stay is brief enough), or they can wear their glasses.

Some students simply can't imagine life without their hair dryers. A few brave souls are willing to try it; the others manage to find the combination of converters and adapters that will allow them to take their blow dryers, hot combs, and curling irons.

An issue that concerned us leaders was the question of portable tape recorders. When students mentioned how many cassettes they were planning to take, we brought the question up for discussion in the group. We felt that putting on a pair of headphones was a way of isolating themselves from the people around them; we found it offensive during group activities and wondered if their hosts would be offended if the Americans retreated to their room to listen to tapes they'd brought from home.

"But the plane ride is seven hours long!" they wailed. "What would we *do* for all that time?" One girl assured us that she simply couldn't get to sleep unless she was listening to music.

Our concern may seem exaggerated—but do you want to walk down a Madrid street leading fifteen kids with headphones on? They wouldn't consider going abroad and wearing blinders, but tape recorders function as status symbols, security blankets, and a socially acceptable way to block out part of the new experience.

In the end, we compromised: during any group activities, the recorders were banned; on long plane, bus, or train rides, they were O.K.; and students agreed to be sensitive to their host families when they listened to tapes during their homestay.

Activity: In a new family

One way to stimulate students to think about the prospect of living with a new family during their homestay is to present a series of vignettes. With a few props, two or three people can illustrate dilemmas that often come up during homestays. The actors can present first the problem, then a way to avoid it, in quick succession; or they can simply present the problem and ask the students for ways to avoid it or resolve it. The actors can speak English or the target language, but be sure everyone can understand what's happening.

Some possible vignettes follow.

Talking it Over

Props: paper plates, silverware. Actors: student, homestay parents.
Setting: dinnertime.

Father: How are you doing, Joanie?

Student [*dejected*]*:* OK.

Mother: Aren't you hungry?

Student: No.

Mother [*worried*]*:* Are you sick?

Student: No.

Father: Is something wrong?

Student [*shrugging*]*:* No. May I go to my room?

Mother: Of course. [*Student leaves.*]

Father: She must not like us.

Mother: Maybe she can't stand my cooking.

[*Now the contrast.*]

Father: How are you doing, Joanie?

Student: Not so good.

Mother: What's wrong? Are you sick?

Student: No. I don't know what's wrong.

Mother: You probably miss your family and friends.

Student: Yeah, I guess so. I haven't gotten any letters at all!

Father: Well, the mail is very slow from the U.S. Besides, of course they miss you, too, even if you don't have any letters yet.

Discussion: What's the problem? What's the difference between the two ways of dealing with it? Why does the first one seem to be the easier way? Why is it more complicated in the end?

Helping Out

Props: paper plates, silverware. Actors: student, homestay parents.
Setting: dinnertime.

Mother: . . . All in all, it was a very tiring day at the office—all finished?

Student: Yes. It was delicious.

Mother [*getting up*]*:* Now I'll do the dishes.

Student: [*handing plate and silverware to mother*]*:* OK [*Turning to father*] Where did you say we're going tomorrow?

[*Now for the contrast.*]

Mother: . . . All in all, it was a very tiring day at the office—all finished?

Student: Yes, thank you. It was delicious.

Mother [*getting up*]*:* Now I'll do the dishes.

Student: Would you like me to help you?

Mother: Oh, no, that's OK.

Student: [*shrugging*]: OK. [*Turning to father*] Where did you say we're going tomorrow?

[*And now for the second contrast.*]

Mother: . . . All in all, it was a very tiring day at the office—all finished?

Student: Yes, thank you. It was delicious.

Mother [*getting up*]*:* Now I'll do the dishes.

Student: No, I'll do the dishes.

Mother: No, no, that's OK.

Student [*getting up, collecting father's plate*]*:* No, you can relax, I'll do them.

Discussion: What are the differences between the second and third scenes? Have you ever had houseguests for a week or more? Did they help out around the house?

Going Out

Props: a note, a pencil. Actors: student, friend, homestay parent.

Friend [*knocking at door*]*:* George?

George [*coming to door*]: Oh, hi, Paul.

Friend: I'm going downtown. Can you go?

George: My family's not here—but I guess it'll be OK.

Friend: Good! Let's go. [*They leave together*].

Parent [*arriving home*]: George? Where can he be? I know he said he'd be home two hours ago. Maybe I should call his leader—or the police? He drives me crazy!

[*Now the contrast.*]

Friend [*knocking at door*]*:* George?

George [*coming to door*]: Oh, hi, Paul.

Friend: I'm going downtown. Can you go?

George: My family's not here, but they probably won't mind. Just a minute, so I can leave a note. When will we be back?

Friend: I don't know.

George: Well, I have to be back by five-thirty, because we eat at six o'clock.

Friend: OK, no problem.

[*George writes note, they leave.*]

Parent [*arriving home*]: George? Where—oh. [*Reading.*] "I've gone downtown with Paul, and I'll be back by five-thirty. Yours, George." How thoughtful!

Discussion: Why was the parent in the first scene so angry?

Activity: Shopping

Shopping, whether for a postcard, a souvenir, or an item of clothing, has great appeal for student travelers. The attraction is understandable: the transaction is usually limited in scope so anyone, even a student with a small vocabulary and limited communicative skills, can carry it off; the purchase sometimes gives students an opening for more extended conversation with a native speaker; and whatever they buy is a tangible trophy, a proof that the transaction was successful.

Since shopping is undeniably a part of the trip, I think it's worthwhile to spend some time in orientation talking about it—what students can get out of it, and how to make it an enjoyable experience without embarrassing themselves or offending anyone in the host culture. Things to consider are: the exchange rate and the host culture's general standard of living (students should be sensitive to the possibility that they can afford luxuries their hosts cannot afford for themselves); the host culture's attitude toward souvenirs (some hosts might feel that a guest's buying souvenirs reflects badly on their hospitality, since it's their place to give their guest presents); and the kinds of souvenirs they buy (hosts might feel offended if they feel that students are buying items that don't represent the host culture).

There are also specific customs that govern shoppers in various kinds of stores. For example, if bargaining is accepted and expected in some situations, explain to the students where and when it's suitable as well as how to go about it without offending the merchant. For another example, in some shops, customers serve themselves, freely examining the merchandise, picking it up and handling it at will, while in other situations unwritten rules require the shopkeeper to serve the customer. Browsers are welcome in some shops and boutiques, but will meet a distinctly cool reception in others. Travelers can learn these customs through trial and error; students will make fewer errors and enjoy shopping more if they know ahead of time that, like eating and other processes that they take for granted, shopping has its own rules that vary from place to place. They can learn the rules by observing other shoppers.

You may be able to suggest typical or inexpensive souvenirs or presents. Many department stores or open-air markets offer more varied gifts or souvenirs than shops or stands that cater specifically to tourists. The students will have a better idea of appropriate items—and appropriate prices—if they wait for a while rather than rushing to buy a lot of things in the first few days. Besides, it'll be easier on them not to have to carry extra things until later in the trip.

Activity: Help your students develop positive attitudes

Most of the orientation activities should raise your students' confidence and make them feel more positive about the trip. At the same time, their nervousness will often come out in negative remarks: "I hear the food over there is gross," or "Janie's host family doesn't even have a car!" Don't let such remarks go by, since often they're a call for reassurance. Pick up on them immediately; try to find out why a student made whatever remark it was, and talk it over. Reassure the students, but at the same time, help them realize how their remarks sound, so they'll begin to listen to themselves. Remind them that they'll be guests in a new country and in their families, and as guests they have an obligation to look for the positive side of whatever they encounter. They're free to *think* whatever they like, but I encourage my students to follow the advice Bambi got: If you can't say anything nice, don't say anything at all.

Activity: **Security**

The truism that the world is much smaller than it once was can affect your students in unexpected ways: political events in faraway places can set off a wave of terrorist activity in a city you're planning to visit. The chances that your students will actually find themselves in the middle of a bombing, hijacking, or kidnapping are really minuscule; the most noticeable effect of terrorism abroad may be that parents or school boards hesitate to allow individuals or groups to travel. If you plan a brief orientation segment on what to do in such an emergency, you may prevent their hesitation from turning into outright refusal.

First of all, students should be discreet: if they happen onto any kind of incident—a scuffle, an accident, a demonstration—they should simply head the other way, resisting their natural urge to find out what's going on. If they should suddenly find themselves in the middle of such an incident, they should try to extricate themselves as quietly and quickly as they can, and make their way to the group's next meeting place, or back to the hotel. They should also be aware of what a consulate is and where the nearest one is, so that they can contact it in case they can't make their way back to the group for any reason.

Another threat to your students' peace of mind is much more likely to be realized: loss of their possessions. Experienced travelers know that American tourists usually stand out visually wherever they go: their physique, gestures, clothes, accessories, hairstyles, walk, and of course language combine to identify them as Americans. Unfortunately, this identifiability (sometimes coupled with carelessness or naivete) makes American tourists easy targets for casual pickpocketing or grab-and-run thievery.

Before students actually pack for the trip, they need to plan what to take and how to carry it to minimize the risk of losing it. They should plan to pack cameras and other valuables out of sight but within reach—their reach: I have read of thieves slitting backpacks, stealing the contents, and making a getaway before the victims even suspect a problem. Urge boys to carry their wallets, passports, and traveler's checks in an inside pocket or in their front pants pocket, not in their hip pocket where even casual pickpockets would find them an easy mark. Girls should take sturdy handbags that they can carry over their shoulders *and tucked under their arms*; they should take care not to let their purses dangle behind them or hang from their arms or wrists.

Of course, some students just won't pay any attention until it's too late. Even after we leaders demonstrated the risks of flimsy shoulder-bags with thin straps, Melinda insisted on bringing her small, elegant shoulder-bag. I was with half the group; we had just been to Notre Dame and were on our way to the Rue de Rivoli on the subway. We all herded into the subway car and then one of the students said, "Isn't this a first-class car?"

"Oh, no," I said confidently—and then realized that it was, indeed, a first-class car; of course we all had second-class tickets. Just at that moment there was a scuffle near the door and a peremptory voice said, "Police!" I thought, They're going to arrest us for having the wrong ticket—but then another voice said, in French, "I didn't do anything!" Realizing vaguely that the situation was more serious than a ticket violation, I said urgently to the students, "*Move back.*"

They obediently shoved each other toward the middle of the car as a young man in a leather jacket flashed an i.d. at me and said, "Police. Do you speak French?"

"A little," I said, not sure what was going on. He pointed to the floor of the subway car, where a fat wallet lay. "Does this belong to you?" he asked.

Melinda, who was standing near me, suddenly gave a little gasp. "My wallet!" she exclaimed, picking it up. The zipper on her purse was gaping open; in the hustle of getting into the car, she hadn't noticed a thing.

The policeman gestured to his partner, who had handcuffed a third young man.

"We saw him follow you into the car," he said. "He just got out of prison for pickpocketing, so we were suspicious, and we ran. We got on just as he opened her handbag. I'm sorry, but you and she will have to come with us to the Palais de Justice to make a deposition. It should only take a little of your time."

So we all got out at the next stop. I told the rest of the group to wait there no matter what, and Melinda and I started back on the same subway line, accompanied by the two plainclothesmen and the guy in handcuffs. The first policeman explained that he and his partner were part of a special squad trying to deal with the hundreds of pickpockets working that subway line. The thieves were rarely armed, since the pickings from tourists were so easy and the penalty for armed robbery was stiff. They made much more money in a month than either his policeman's pay or my teaching salary.

In a garret of the Palais de Justice, he threw his revolver into a drawer and then typed our deposition on a creaky old typewriter, while his partner interrogated the suspect in the next room. When I asked how many thieves they caught, he sighed.

"That man just spent a year in prison," he said. "He went right back to it. We'll be here until late tonight, filling out all the papers in this case."

When we got back to the group in the subway, they had been waiting for an hour and a half.

"We wanted to leave," they said, "but we knew you'd kill us, so we waited. What happened, anyway? Were they arresting Melinda, or what?"

Kill them? I wanted to kiss each and every one of them. Without understanding what was going on, they had sacrificed half of one precious afternoon in Paris because they knew it was an emergency. It turned out that Melinda had just cashed $300 in travelers' checks; the money, the rest of her checks, and her passport were all in the fat wallet on the floor of the subway car.

It's probably useful to tell students explicitly that no possession is worth a risk to their safety. On the platform of the Paris métro, Cindy let go of her ticket, which wafted out over the tracks. Karen Libby, a leader, stopped Cindy as she lunged after the ticket. Cindy broke free and said, "It's OK, I can climb down and get it—" This time Karen grabbed her and hung on until she could explain to Cindy how dangerous the tracks were. Later, Cindy was telling me about the incident. "If I had been killed," she asked, "would you have called my parents right away to tell them, or would you have waited until the group got home?"

Activity: **Orientation dinner**

A sit-down meal of foreign food for small groups of students may be their only chance to try out what they've learned during orientation—and their foreign language—in a real (or at least realistic) situation before they leave on the trip. So many cultural values are centered on food and hospitality that mealtimes may be some of the most intimidating moments of their homestay; they'll welcome a chance to rehearse before they confront those moments on their own.

The dinner needn't be elaborate, nor should it mean enormous amounts of work for you, but it should be at your house, if possible; if that's not practical, it should be at someone else's house—but not at school, as school can't seem like a family setting. The meal should be formal enough so that the students don't feel completely at home, since they won't feel that way at first during their homestays. This may sound cruel; it isn't. This dinner, like many of the role-play activities, is a chance for the students to meet a challenge before the trip begins, and so build their confidence. I've found that inviting the students in groups of eight to ten, serving food that was unfamiliar to them, and speaking the host language during the meal established enough formality so that I could concentrate on putting them at their ease and keeping the conversation rolling.

It's important to serve at least some food that's new to most of the students, so they'll learn to react gracefully to unfamiliar dishes. For recipe ideas, look through international cookbooks, or ask around among colleagues or friends who've traveled to where you'll be going. Be sure to look for easy recipes that can be made in quantity ahead of time and refrigerated or frozen. There's no need for you to do the cooking: enlist students, their parents, anyone you can find. You may be able to buy some dishes: phone restaurants, bakeries or caterers, explain your needs, and see if they can help. Include this dinner in your budget, because otherwise it could be very expensive or very time-consuming for you. Parents and students are usually quick to see its value and approve its inclusion in the group's budget.

Students' reactions to the dinner may vary enormously. Some may not say a word unless they're addressed directly, but others will find, to their surprise, that the new situation is in some way liberating rather than intimidating, and they'll be able to talk quite comfortably. Along the way they'll make some discoveries about the way of life they'll be sharing: after I'd served potato soup, then quiche (not Swiss, but at least vaguely French), and salad, one girl asked, "Do they really eat their meals in *parts* like this?"

You may want to plan some orientation activity for after dinner. If your students are preparing projects, this is a good time for them to present their projects to the rest of the group: as a sympathetic audience (since presumably they'll all have to present their own projects sooner or later), the other students can give encouragement and at the same time suggest ways to make the presentations clearer or livelier.

Activity: **Culture shock**

Books have been written about culture shock, but your students won't have read them, so it's very important to tell them *and their parents* about culture shock: recognizing it will help the students get through it, and in the meantime the parents won't get so frantic if their children experience it.

How you choose to present it is up to you. I wrote about it in a bulletin to the students and their parents, which we discussed later:

Culture Shock

If after a few days in Geneva you begin to feel angry/overwhelmed/blue, if you start to feel that your Swiss brother/sister/mother/father is babying you/mean to you/neglecting you, that the Swiss as a nationality are cold/overly sentimental/sarcastic/stubborn—if in general you start to feel uncomfortable and miserable, **take heart**. You'll be experiencing **culture shock.**

Culture shock is the perfectly natural reaction to the fact that you won't feel *at home*— with your new family, with the language, with the way things look, smell, taste, sound. It's called culture shock because it can come very suddenly: one minute everything's fine, the next minute you're ready to catch the first plane home.

When it hits you, don't panic. Remember that it happens to everybody in some form, that it doesn't last long, and that you'll laugh about it when it's all over. Remember, too, that no one's to blame: your Swiss family is doing their best for you, and storekeepers, bus drivers, and other people you don't know are just doing their jobs as they always have. So this feeling's not their fault or yours or anyone's: it just happens.

If you feel it coming on, **call us**. We're there to help. If there's a specific problem or misunderstanding, we may be able to smooth it out for you. If you simply want to talk things over with someone (and it does help), let us know.

I understand that you'll be talking to other people in the group, but if there's *any* problem, I would like to know about it, since it's probably a question of communication or of crossed expectation. It's not fair to you or to your Swiss family if you suffer in silence (or, worse, suffer loudly to your friends in the group, who can't do anything about it except suffer, too).

In our discussion, we reemphasized that students shouldn't hesitate to call on us if they began feeling any of the symptoms of culture shock. Knowing that it's sometimes hard for adolescents to admit that they need help, I told them, "You don't have to explain. Just give us a call, and say 'Culture shock.' We'll take it from there." We chartered a bus to take us from Brattleboro to Logan Airport in Boston, and as we emerged from the Callahan Tunnel and turned into the airport, I could hear excited comments from the back of the bus:

"Is this the airport?"

"Yeah, I think so."

"Which building?"

"I don't know. Let's ask."

"Hey, Mrs. Cassidy! Which building's the airport?"

"It's *all* airport."

A few seconds of silence, then several voices shouted at once.

"Culture shock! Culture shock!"

10

Get Set—

The funds have been raised, orientation sessions are nearly over. Only three weeks or a month remain before you leave. It's time to think about last-minute preparations that will make departure smoother, communication with home clearer, and your administrative tasks easier.

Final permission form

The final permission form is a quasi-legal document in which each student's parents or guardians give formal permission for the students to leave on the trip. They express their understanding of the conditions for participation in the group, accept responsibility for their child's behavior, and agree to pay for the child's immediate return if, in your judgment, the child violates the conditions of participation. Finally, they give you permission to act *in loco parentis* in case of a medical emergency.

It's a good idea to have your school's lawyer check a draft of whatever form you use, to be sure that legally it says what you want it to say. Of course, your school may have a standard form for you to use. Here is a sample form:

To whom it may concern:

I hereby give my child, _____ ,

permission to participate in the _____

_____ .

I have read and understood the Conditions of Participation; I agree that if, in the

judgment of _____

_____ ,

the leader(s), my child violates those conditions, my child may be sent home immediately at
my expense; furthermore, I am responsible for any expenses incurred by my child.

Further, I hereby authorize _____

(or _____), the leader(s),
to exercise his/her discretion in authorizing any medical or surgical treatment which he/she
may deem necessary for my child.

Signed, _____

Signed and sworn to before me this _____ day of _____ , 19___ , at _____ .

_____
Notary Public

In order to ensure that medical authorities will recognize this permission as legally
valid, it's worthwhile to ask the parents to have their signatures notarized. Some of the
parents themselves may be notaries; if they can bring their seals to a parents' meeting, the
whole process is simplified. Otherwise the parents must find a notary on their own, but
knowing that their children can get emergency medical treatment will make it worthwhile.

You can also record each student's passport number and traveler's check numbers on
the back of this form. A student who loses either his passport or his checks will be able to get
them more easily if he knows their numbers.

Medical insurance forms

Be sure you have blank forms for your medical insurance policy. It's much easier to get all the information and signatures you need in order to collect if you have the forms with you. Take at least one for each student: you may not need any at all, but food poisoning or a contagious disease sweeping the group will make you glad to have enough forms for everyone.

Miscellaneous medical details

Have your students *enter in their passports* any essential medical information (see numbers 2 and 3 on the information form), your name and where you can be reached at each step of the journey; perhaps they can write the information on a separate piece of paper attached to the inside of the passport. In case of emergency, if the student is unconscious or unable to speak for himself or herself, police or medical officials will check the student's passport. You may be spared a lot of anxiety if authorities know where to reach you promptly, and you can gather the facts and judge the situation for yourself before getting in touch with the parents; it will be easier for them to get news from you than from a stranger.

Students who wear contact lenses should also put a note saying so in their passports. Contact lenses can be dangerous if left in too long, and if the student is incapacitated, the note can alert a doctor to the problem.

Of course these measures will be useless unless the students carry their passports with them all the time. Urge them to do so: they may need them for identification, and the passports are safer with them than in a hotel room. Even during their homestays, students should carry their passports for identification.

Tell the students that if they're not feeling well, you need to know about it. Equip yourself with Band-aids for small cuts or blisters, Dramamine or another nonprescription remedy for travel sickness, and (especially if you're going somewhere where the diet is radically different) Kaopectate or another antidiarrheal medicine. If the students can come to you for relatively minor physical problems, they'll be more likely to come to you for more serious ones.

Traveler's checks

Students may need guidance in purchasing traveler's checks. First of all, explain what the checks are, and urge the students to buy them instead of taking cash.

You may want to limit the amount of money that each student takes, in order to limit the amount of time and attention the students spend shopping. The limit would depend on how long your trip is, where you're going, and what expenses the students will have to pay out of pocket. During both Swiss exchanges (the first in 1979, when the Swiss franc was worth about $.67, and in 1981, when it had dropped to about $.50), I advised students to take no more than $300.00 for the three weeks of our stay. Of course, in both of those cases the host families took care of nearly all the students' expenses. Some students spent as little as $150.00 on snacks, film, entertainment, souvenirs for themselves, and presents for people at home.

If you do wish to set a limit on spending money, be sure to talk it over with the parents. In this, as in other questions, they'll almost certainly support your decision when they understand your thinking.

Though traveler's checks are available in some foreign currencies, there's no reason to buy these rather than checks in dollars, which are accepted everywhere that the others would be. Furthermore, the students would pay a premium to convert their dollars into checks in francs, pesos, or marks, and if they didn't cash all the checks, they would have to pay another premium to reconvert them into dollars.

Your own finances

Since you have to carry both group funds and your own money with you on the trip, buying one kind of traveler's check for the group funds and another brand for your personal funds is an easy way to keep them separate.

You'll need to keep careful track of the group funds. It's possible to develop elaborate and detailed systems to do this; I simply note down everything I spend from the group funds. I also keep receipts as records of the larger transactions.

Presents for the homestay families

Students who'll be staying with homestay families should bring some fairly substantial present to the family. If the students have been corresponding with their families, or if their counterparts have already visited, they may have at least an idea of their families' interests and lifestyle. If they don't know their families at all, finding an appropriate gift will be harder.

A FEW RULES OF THUMB: the present should be easy to transport safely. Airlines are not gentle with the luggage entrusted to their care, so it's better not to risk taking anything very fragile.

The more of the student that goes into the gift, the better. A Finnish student who stayed with my family sent us an album of photos of the island where she spent her summers. She'd made the album itself, taken the pictures, and labeled each one to explain what it was and why it was important to her. The album was beautiful in itself, and (even more importantly) through it she shared her life with us.

Even if students can't make presents themselves, a gift that has some meaning for the student will touch the host family—if the student explains why he chose it. Books with pictures of familiar places or handicrafts produced by local artisans might be suitable.

If students are considering a gift for their host family's house, something that can be brought out for special occasions is preferable to a present that demands to be used every day or displayed on a wall; that way, even if the gift doesn't fit the decor of the house, it can give great pleasure to the family.

Students should steer clear of products that are marketed specifically for tourists in their area, unless the products have exceptional quality and interest. In general, things produced for the tourist trade don't do justice to what the area has to offer.

Some suggestions for presents:

- a book of photos of the U.S. or of your region or community;
- an engagement calendar with artwork or photos from your area;
- a tablecloth, placemats, or table napkins, especially if they're made locally;
- a wooden cutting board, trivet, salad bowl or cheese board;

- a trivet, small box, or vase made of wood, metal, or stone (or of ceramic, if it can be packed safely);

- candlesticks, bowls, or other accessories made of brass or pewter;

- luxury food from your region: though fruits and vegetables don't travel well and may encounter problems at the border, nuts, candy, or preserves don't have those problems;

- a record, especially if the student knows his hosts' tastes. Records require very careful packing;

- a small antique.

While you and the students are looking for presents, you may also want to look ahead to a final party for the homestay families, and get some favors or small flags to help establish the atmosphere. The local Chamber of Commerce may be willing to donate suitable materials. At the same time, some local merchant or manufacturer may donate a small present for each family, to be distributed at that final party. These gifts should *not* take the place of presents from individual students to their families.

Students may also want to take copies of favorite recipes. They can prepare dishes for their own host families or for the final party for all the host families. The ingredients should be staples, since brand-name ingredients may not be readily available where you're going.

Prepare your students to keep journals

Keeping a journal during the trip will add depth to your students' experience. A journal can help them catch each impression on the fly; without one, events and their reactions to them have a way of blending into one another and blurring in the students' memories. For some students the journal is an invaluable outlet for their feelings, which otherwise might threaten to overwhelm them. If they wish to share their journals with friends and family, the journals will show what the trip meant to them with a freshness and immediacy that even photos can't capture. Lisa wrote about our final morning in Paris:

> Maggie called around ¼ to 7:00 Kelly freaked right out when the phone rang. She sat up and said "Oh my god what's that" I said the telephone It was Andrea. Kelly got up first to take a shower & there was no water in the tub— because everyone was trying to use it. So I went down the hall to ask Dan & Mick what was going on in their room. They didn't have hot water either. Finally, after Kelly had washed her hair in the sink, the hot water worked. Mickey called to say that their hot water was working. I took a shower, bath. The bath looks like this:

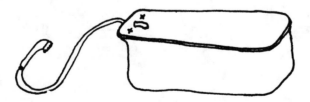

> You must take a shower w/ the shower head in your hand. The shower is called a douche here.

Students recognize their journals' value—after the fact; but they need strong persuasion to begin keeping them. For my students, credit was an effective persuader: turning in their journals was a requirement for obtaining credit for the trip. A local book press donated blank books in various colors, handsomely embossed with the company name, so the students didn't even have to buy their own journals; we distributed them at a meeting with Gordon Hayward, a freelance writer who teaches English at our school. He showed them the very lively journals he and his wife had kept during a trip to Greece. Seeing his journal and receiving their own at this meeting shortly before we left kindled the students' enthusiasm for the idea of keeping their own journals.

Gordon showed them that journals can be more than writing: they can be collections of things that remind a traveler, more strongly than words can do, what a given moment was really like. A ticket stub from a museum, a check from a restaurant, a wrapper from a particular kind of candy, a matchbook cover, a label from a wine bottle—all bring back with a rush a place, a group of people, a conversation, even a smell or a feeling. He underlined the importance of keeping up with a journal faithfully. Unless the objects are glued in and labeled promptly, the journal will never take shape; it will end up a sad jumble of unrecorded memories and debris. Gordon also put postcards in his journal. He explained that they were available on the spot (there's no wait for them to be developed) and usually better than his photos; besides, they save him from spending a lot of time taking pictures instead of looking at things directly, for his own pleasure. Postcards are also less expensive than photos, especially since people tend to take a lot of shots of the same thing to be sure of getting the shot they want. Of course, there will be no postcards of the group itself, the host families or their homes, and the students will surely want to take their own pictures of those people and places.

Packing: help students understand its importance

Packing—even thinking about packing—can make the students realize for the first time that they're really going abroad. Even after they've been through hours of orientation, it shocks them to look at their closets and their dressers and understand suddenly that they'll be able to take only a small portion of what they see there.

Their reaction is natural, when looked at in the light of their experience. First of all, Americans like to travel by car; even if they take a plane or bus, they usually drive or are driven to the airport or bus station and then they're met by a car at their destination. Result: luggage is generally limited only by how much will fit into a car—not by how much one person can carry. Secondly, American teenagers change their clothes all the time, and never wear the same thing two days in a row if they can help it. And finally, Americans wash their clothes often, and because they know that they'll be washing their clothes soon, they take little care to keep them neat and clean beyond one wearing.

International travel forces upon American students the same circumstances faced by people in other countries all the time: a limited number of clothes to choose from and laundry facilities that are expensive or inconvenient. Before a trip it's hard to persuade students that they won't need to take very many clothes: if they choose clothes that are easy to care for, and then take care of them (by washing them when necessary, hanging them up and airing them between wearings), they'll be surprised to see how few clothes they really need. Experience is the best teacher, but you can help by providing a list of packing suggestions and by organizing a luggage hike, which will show them what it will really feel like to carry everything they've packed.

Packing lists

Here's a packing list designed for a three-week stay in Switzerland in winter. Adjust it for a visit of different duration in a different climate.

Clothes (for women)

□ 2 skirts, one casual, one dressy *or* one dress and one skirt

□ 2 pairs dressy pants (not corduroy jeans)

□ 2 pairs jeans or corduroy jeans

□ 1 pair pants to ski in

□ 3 blouses or shirts, ranging from casual to dressy

□ 1 turtleneck, cotton or light wool

□ 1 heavy (ski) sweater

□ 4 or 5 sets of underwear *(not more;* you can wash these by hand, and you won't want to carry them, clean or dirty)

□ nightgown, bathrobe

□ 1 set long underwear (for skiing)

□ socks, tights, pantyhose

□ 1 parka or windbreaker (for skiing)

□ 1 coat or raincoat for city (it should be made for fog and rain as well as cold)

□ 1 pair of boots

□ 1 pair of casual shoes

□ 1 pair of dressy shoes

□ gloves or mittens

□ hat (for skiing)

Clothes (for men)

□ 1 raincoat or overcoat

□ 1 sports jacket

□ 1 necktie

□ 1 dress shirt

□ 2 sports shirts

□ 2 pairs dress pants

□ 2 pairs *nice* jeans

□ 1 or 2 dressy sweaters

□ 1 heavy sweater (for skiing)

□ 1 parka or windbreaker (for skiing)

□ 2 turtlenecks/rugby shirts/T-shirts

□ 2 pairs comfortable walking shoes or 1 pair shoes, 1 pair boots

□ 1 pair dressy shoes

☐ 1 hat (for skiing)

☐ gloves or mittens

☐ pajamas, bathrobe

☐ 4 sets underwear

☐ 1 set long underwear (for skiing)

☐ 4 pairs socks

☐ shaving kit

☐ proper belt (preferably one for all pants)

Nonclothing items (for everyone—pick and choose):

☐ passport

☐ traveler's checks

☐ journal

☐ toothbrush and paste

☐ shampoo, cosmetics, deodorant, etc., but in small packages

☐ washcloth and small towel, for use on the plane

☐ soap if your skin demands a particular kind

☐ camera, film

☐ airmail stationery and envelopes (small quantity)

☐ sanitary supplies

☐ portable hairdryer (*only* if you can't live without it), and converter or adapter for it

☐ razor (with adapter or converter if it's electric). Disposable razors are lightweight, inexpensive, and convenient

☐ shaving cream

☐ medication if you need it, especially for allergies. Medication should be in the original container, clearly labeled

☐ sunglasses

☐ a couple of Band-aids (not a whole box)

☐ present for Swiss family

☐ address book

☐ tiny notebook for new words, addresses, directions, messages

How to pack

It's important to have a balanced load, so encourage students not to take one huge, clumsy, heavy suitcase. Preferable would be either two small suitcases (one small enough to go on the plane as hand luggage), or one suitcase and a small backpack or shoulderbag; if a student decides to take a backpack big enough to check, it shouldn't have a fragile frame that could be damaged if it's thrown around.

In whatever combination, students should have one sturdy piece of luggage, which they'll check, and one smaller piece, as light as possible, to take on the plane. In this they should pack:

- □ a sweater (sometimes it's cold on the plane)
- □ toothbrush and paste, washcloth and towel
- □ one change of underwear, in case checked luggage gets lost
- □ camera and film
- □ passport and airline ticket
- □ traveler's checks, but *not* the receipt for them; that should always be packed separately, in case they get lost. If students carry the checks in a purse or wallet, the receipt can go in their hand luggage
- □ journal
- □ something to read (a magazine or novel) in case it's hard to sleep on the plane

If the students wear some of their heavy clothing, they won't have to carry it. At the same time, they should certainly be able to carry it all, in case they're too warm wearing it.

The luggage hike

The luggage hike is a tradition at the Experiment in International Living. Students come to New England for two weeks of language training before they go abroad, and near the end of their stay they pack their luggage with everything they haven't yet sent home, and carry it along a set route—a rehearsal for the first time the group is rushing to catch a train. The hike ends at the mailroom, where there are boxes, mailing labels, and people to help the Experimenters pack the things they've decided they can bear to send home after all. One of the Experiment's mottos is, "Learn by doing." The luggage hike teaches students that they may be able to pack a lot into two small suitcases—but they may not want to carry it all.

Is it worth your group's time to have a luggage hike? It depends on whether they'll need to carry their bags during the trip. If you're going to be met at an airport by homestay families, and returned to the airport by those same families, there's evidently no need for the group to practice carrying their luggage around. On the other hand, if the students will be carrying their luggage from an airport to a bus to a hotel to a train station, or if they'll be carrying their bags on public transportation *even once,* a luggage hike is worthwhile. A group can only move as fast as its slowest member, so all it takes is one student carrying too much to slow down the entire group.

My students didn't believe we'd really go through with a luggage hike. "Aw, c'mon," they said, "we get the idea. We don't really have to do it, right?" Wrong. The week before we left, we met at school with suitcases, totes, backpacks, duffels, and even a pair of skis, and tramped outside into the snow, around the outside of the building, and in by another door. It turned out that the hike was much easier and shorter than our first trek through the Paris subway, but as it was, the walk was long enough to impress some of the students. Others hadn't really packed everything they intended to take with them, so the hike didn't test their stamina as it should have.

If you organize a luggage hike, make it longer than you think your group will actually need to walk with their luggage. The extra steps will help save some sore shoulders and frazzled nerves during the trip. Lead the group up and down stairs, through doors, and over some bumpy ground: some students buy wheels for outsize suitcases, thinking they can simply roll their luggage along; they forget to take bumpy sidewalks and stairs into consideration.

After the hike, talk seriously with the students who fell far behind the group. Go over the packing list with them to find out what they're taking that they might not need. One girl said thoughtfully, "Well, maybe I could take one less sweater."

"How many are you taking?" I asked.

"Five," she said.

Individual interviews—again

If you don't get much chance to see the students except during group meetings, you may want to set up another series of individual interviews. You can double-check each student's permission form, medical form, passport number, and other administrative details; you can ask each student what he's taking to his homestay family, and you can ask for or convey any information that might be too personal for a group meeting. For example, girls may wonder what to do about disposing of tampons or sanitary napkins during their periods. They can avoid needless anxiety and embarrassment if you provide the vocabulary they need and suggest that they ask their homestay mothers or sisters what to do.

You may also want to bring up sexual conduct, especially if you think that your students are sexually active or if the mores of the country where you're going are very different from those of your community. Students will probably appreciate your warning them about potentially embarrassing situations before they find themselves in the middle of one.

Draw up an itinerary and a list of names
and addresses

Your communication with everyone will be much easier if you draw up a detailed itinerary (complete with plans for departure and return) and a list of the names, addresses, and phone numbers of:

□ the students

□ their counterparts

□ yourself

□ your counterpart abroad

□ a school official

□ hotels where you'll be staying

If you'll be away from major cities, you could include a map indicating where you'll be.

Make plenty of copies of this information, and distribute copies to everyone involved: students, parents, school officials, even local news media.

Perhaps a colleague or a student group would be willing to put up a map at school and indicate the group's progress on it. "It's October second; they're in Heidelberg."

Arrange communication with home

It will set the parents' minds at ease to know that the group has arrived safely at its destination. Arrange to call or cable to some central location; either the parents can call that central phone, or, if it's more convenient, they can set up a phone tree to pass the news. Setting up a phone tree is a good idea, anyway, in case there's something the parents need to know—like when you'll arrive home if the plane's delayed.

If a local radio station shows an interest in the trip, the station manager or news director might be willing to call the group (or have you call the station) and broadcast the interview as a feature or on the local news.

Prepare for emergencies

Talk with an administrator at your school about what to do in an emergency (see "Emergencies," Chapter 12). If possible, arrange for money to be sent if you need it; your emergency fund should cover your immediate needs until extra funds can be sent.

Meet with the students and parents one last time

A week or two before you leave, meet once more with the students and their parents. Starting with when and where you'll meet on the day of your departure, go through the trip step by step, outlining what the group will be doing in as much detail as seems suitable. You can also reiterate your rules and expectations for the students. Leave time for questions as you go along.

Take a few minutes to warn the parents—gently—that their children may seem a little like strangers when they first return from the trip. They may not believe you (the students almost certainly won't believe you, either), but hearing it will at least make them think about the question. No one can predict exactly how such a trip will affect someone, but most students become much more aware of the world around them and much more confident in dealing with it. In some the changes are even visible: when we returned from Switzerland, several teachers remarked that one student just *looked different,* in some indefinable way.

At times students change in ways that parents find disconcerting. One girl, who'd always been close to her parents, came back in the throes of adolescent rebellion. Moody and uncommunicative, she seemed to reject their religion and values as well as their attempts to talk with her. Months later, when the family had more or less returned to normal, her mother told me, "I wish we'd had some warning. We probably had to go through that with her at some point, but we certainly weren't expecting it *then.* Three weeks is no time at all, and parents think the relationship they have with their child is like a rubber band, that it'll stretch over any distance. It's just not so; at that age things happen *fast,* and we just weren't ready." Perhaps the parents will be ready if you talk over with them the possibility that when their children come back, they won't seem quite the same. One way or another they'll probably have grown up, often in unexpected ways.

And that's it. Now all you have to do is make up lesson plans for your substitute, figure out how your family will get along without you, pack, answer your students' last-minute questions—and go.

11
GO!

As the students gather at their departure point, check to be sure that each student has his or her passport and traveler's checks. Don't take yes for an answer; insist on seeing the goods.

Once you're actually on the road or in the air, life becomes a lot simpler. It's no use worrying about whether you should have done this or that. All you need to do is keep in touch with your students, keep track of the group funds, and—most of all—keep your sense of humor.

Keep in touch with your students

It's essential, all through the trip, that you stay in touch with your students—that you know what they're going through and how it's affecting them. Some will come to you on their own, eager to share their experiences; others would never think of doing so, but you should try to be aware of everyone. If you establish the habit of going around to all the students to find out how they're doing, your interest will seem natural to them. If you wait until something goes wrong, your curiosity will seem intrusive and they may resent it.

The count-off—a way to keep track of your students

Whenever the group assembles, you need to be sure everyone's there before you set off again. If more than 12 students are milling around, it's easy to lose track of exactly who really is there. To make the nose count more efficient, each of my students has a number:

during the last orientation session before we leave, I ask them to line up alphabetically and count off in that order. From then on, any time I need to check that everyone's together, I simply ask them to count off. Students quickly learn their own numbers and those of whoever precedes and follows them.

At first the students think this system is silly, but they soon see that it works well—if everyone is paying attention. They take it upon themselves to straighten out anyone who daydreams or forgets his or her number, since that person is holding up the whole group. The system relieves you of a time-consuming and sometimes irritating task; at the same time, it forces the students to be responsible to each other rather than only to you, thus reinforcing their group spirit.

Prepare for jet lag and fatigue

Travel is tiring for everybody, but even more so for adolescents, who often push themselves too far without realizing it.

Jet lag seems to fade more quickly if travelers force themselves to adapt to the new time as soon as possible. This means that if you're traveling from west to east, even if you miss a night's sleep, try to put off catching up on the missed night until it really is night, local time. Move at a slow pace through the day; take a brief nap, if need be; go to bed at 6:00 in the evening—but try to sleep during the night, so that the next morning you'll be in step with local time.

To make the adaptation easier, keep the group's activities to a minimum for the first 24 hours or so. Let them explore the neighborhood around the hotel; encourage them to write a first round of postcards, pointing out that they won't have much time later on.

Teenagers often fail to realize how fatigue can affect their digestion, so they can easily get sick from overloading their systems. A hamburger and an order of fries or a few slices of pizza may appeal to their longing for a taste of home, but greasy or spicy foods are likely to upset their stomachs. Urge them to eat very lightly until their bodies get adjusted to their new schedule and surroundings. Liquids—especially tea, bottled fruit juice, mineral water, and soft drinks—are usually easy on the stomach and will help them avoid the diarrhea or constipation that can accompany a sudden change of diet or schedule.

After all the last-minute rush to leave, the students' spontaneous wonder and excitement at the beginning of a trip are the best antidote to your own fatigue and the small voice that asks, "What have I gotten myself into?" After a fitful sleep over the Atlantic, Dan and I awoke bleary-eyed, to find several of our students eagerly taking photos of the sunrise. One of them came over to us and gestured out the window toward the layers of pink and orange light on the horizon. "I think that's the most beautiful thing I've ever seen," he said.

12

Out on the Town

If you planned your group's activities before you left (see Chapter 4), your students should have a fairly clear idea of what they'll be doing each day. This chapter simply suggests ways to make a city visit smoother for them and for you.

Make sure students know where they belong

All students should have the hotel's name, address and phone number with them so that if they get separated, they'll be able to find their way back. If possible, give a city map to each student or small group of students and make sure they know where the hotel is on the map. They should also carry their passports with them as identification.

Whenever students go off on their own or in small groups during their unstructured time, ask them where they intend to go, at least in general terms. Write it down, so that if they don't return when they're supposed to, you'll know where to begin looking for them.

Always give clear directions as to when and exactly where the group will meet next. I say "exactly where" because if the group is to meet "back at the hotel at six o'clock," some students may be in their rooms, some may be in the lobby, some may be standing out front —and someone will have to waste a lot of time running around to assemble them.

Help them use public transportation

The students will find most public transportation easy to use once they get the hang of it, and going through it with you at least once will help them get the hang of it easily. One of your first group outings, after the students have settled into their hotel rooms, could take you to some landmark or tourist site via public transit. Very tired students can return immediately to the hotel, leaving further discoveries for when they're fresher; those with more energy can explore the area before finding their way back to the hotel.

Before you set out on this first expedition, ask at your hotel how to get public transit maps for your students. Have them locate the hotel (marking its location for further reference), locate your destination, and figure out the best way to get from one to the other. Explain the system of payment (tickets, tokens, or change), give them the vocabulary they'll need, and then stand by as they pay and board the bus or tram or subway.

All of this will take time. Of course it would be more efficient if you just bought tickets and handed them out, but the sooner the students learn to take responsibility for themselves, the more they'll learn from the trip and enjoy it.

Guide the students in observing the new culture

I'll discuss three ways of helping your students look at and enjoy their new surroundings. The first is to help them psychologically, the second is to help them organize their time, and the third is to provide them with an observation guide.

You can help them focus their attention: talk over what they're going to see (and suggest things to look for), talk with them as they're going through the activity (if you're around), and then ask them to share their experiences afterward.

One of our group excursions in Switzerland was to the château in the village of Gruyère. Because I'd never visited the castle (or done any research!), I couldn't prepare my students for the visit by giving them information about the castle or suggesting specific things to look at. As a result, they raced through the castle, stopping only when some artifact snagged their attention. On the other hand, our visit to the Rolex watch factory was so successful partly because M. Troesch and I had told the students that Rolex watches are known around the world for their precision and reliability; furthermore, the company rarely allowed students to tour the factory. As they followed the watchmaking process through the factory, the students saw how the precise handwork, the elaborate tests after each step in the watches' assembly, and even the building's design all contributed to the quality of the finished product. Without any introduction, they could easily have assumed that all of those things were part of watchmaking everywhere—as they may have assumed Gruyère's breathtaking site and frescoes are common to castles.

Talking with students during an activity also helps them sharpen their perceptions. At a museum, ask them what work of art they like best, and why; ask whether or not they'd like to live in the palace you're touring, and why or why not; show them your own discoveries of the moment; help them compare and contrast two similar things.

Finally, talk with them to follow up on their experiences, especially the ones you didn't share. Don't overlook their interactions with other people: one of my students was so taken aback by the inexplicable rage of a ticket-seller at the Louvre that she had trouble thinking about what else she'd seen there. She needed reassurance that she would be able to talk with other native French-speakers without infuriating them, too.

Chapter 4 suggests ways to organize the group's activities to keep the students interested. It's up to them to organize their structured time, but you can encourage them to combine their shopping and people-watching with other activities if you prepare a worksheet of possibilities arranged like a Chinese menu, with directions to choose (for example), five items from Part A and five items from Part B. As they complete the activities they choose, the students can check them off and answer the questions. For a more extended stay, the list could include more items.

WORKSHEET FOR PARIS

Part A

Choose five of the following activities. Put a check next to each activity you did, and answer the questions.

_____ Buy *Pariscope* (weekly tourist guide)

_____ Order a drink in a cafe. What did you order? _____

How much did it cost? _____

_____ Ask someone for directions. To where? _____

_____ Buy a postcard of a monument or tourist site. Which one did you choose? _____

_____ Buy a souvenir for someone. What did you buy? _____

_____ Take the subway or bus. From where did you take it? _____

Where did you go? _____

_____ Order a meal in a restaurant (NOT McDonald's or a fast-food place). What did you

order? _____

_____ Visit a department store. How is it different from an American department

store? _____

_____ Buy the ingredients for a picnic in a supermarket or in small neighborhood

stores. What did you buy? _____

_____ Where did you have the picnic? _____

_____ Ask a stranger for the time. What was the person's reaction? _____

_____ Try one dish in an ethnic (neither French nor American) restaurant. What did you

try? _____ Would you order it again? _____

WORKSHEET FOR PARIS

Part B

Visit five of the following sites. Put a check next to each site you have visited, and answer the questions.

———— Le Jardin des Tuileries: What did you see there?

_____

———— Le Jeu de Paume: Name three artists whose work you saw there.

_____

———— Le Musée de Cluny: What was your favorite sight there?

_____

———— Le Centre Beaubourg: What exhibitions did you see?

_____

Did you like the building? ———— Why or why not? _____

_____

———— Le Musée des Invalides: What was the building used for originally?

_____

———— La Tour Eiffel: What landmarks could you see from the top?

_____

———— Le Sacré Coeur: How did you get there?

_____

———— Le Panthéon: What names did you recognize?

_____

The following cultural observation guide comes from the Ibero-American Cultural Exchange Program, which kindly gave me permission to publish it here. The questions in this guide are open-ended, to allow students to draw their own conclusions over time. You can adapt these questions, written specifically for Mexico, to your host country.

CULTURAL OBSERVATION GUIDE

FIRST IMPRESSIONS
and how they change

When you arrive in Mexico, write down, probably just before you go to bed, what your first impressions have been and if they affect how you feel.

ASSIGNMENTS
on your trip

The following assignments are to do while you are in Mexico. They do not have to be done the first week but keep reading over the list of activities so that by the time the trip is over you have completed any *15* out of the *23* assignments. Some will be easier for some of you to complete than others because of where you are staying while in Mexico.

1. Clothing

Take some time, standing on the street corner, in a cafe, or in the park and observe the way the Mexicans dress. Take note of the most common articles.

> *Examples:* headgear
> shoes/handbags
> dresses/slacks
> shirts/blouses/sweaters
> other garments/jewelry

Try to answer the following questions about what you have observed:

1. Is the Mexican dress as stylish as you expected? What did you expect?

2. Who was not stylish in your opinion? (Can you make a general statement about this?)

3. Does the dress indicate social class?

4. Compare what you see in Mexico to what you see in the U.S.

2. Food: types

What are the markets like? Are there supermarkets? Try to find the bean section someday when you are in the market and see how many kinds of beans there are. Do you recognize them? What kind of generalization can you make about the variety? Can you ask someone to explain why there are so many kinds and how they are used?

3. Individuality and conformity

Observe the following: see if you can see examples of individuality or lack of it in the following areas of Mexican life.

cars
drivers
clothing
people's public behavior
food
architecture
home furnishings

4. Jobs

Keep a list of services and jobs you notice and also that you hear about. Notice those especially unfamiliar to you. If possible try to find out what the pay is for each job so that you can make a comparison.

5. Signs

Keep track of all the different directional signs that you see and what their function is. Are they similar to or different from those in the United States? Are they followed by the people?

6. Cemeteries and churchs

See what you can find out about Mexican people by these examples. For instance, inscriptions on grave stones or elaborate or simple churches. Are churches crowded? (Are men, women, and children in attendance?)

7. Families

Conversation (is there much?)

Do children and young adults (like yourselves) do as they please?

How do young people act in front of their parents, other adults?

What is the typical behavior for a young person?

What is the typical behavior for the parent?

Are these qualities different from most U.S. families? Are they different from your own family?

8. Children

What are they like?

9. **Language:** formality

   a. What is the distinction between the use of *tú* and *Ud.?*

   b. How long does it take before a teenager will address one of his or her friends as *tú?*

   c. How long does it take for that teenager to address an adult acquaintance as *tú?*

   d. Does the teenager with whom you are staying address his parents' friends as *tú?* If so, are they close friends?

   e. How does one decide on the proper occasion to use *tú?*

   f. What do the *tú* and *usted* forms indicate to you about the Mexican culture?

   g. Do we have this distinction in the U.S.? Do you think it makes a difference? How?

10. **Handshaking**

    Try to observe when people shake hands and see who shakes hands with whom. Ask people to tell you if you aren't sure what their opinion is of handshaking.

11. **Social gathering places**

    If you have the opportunity to go to a café, see what you can see. Who speaks to whom? How? What people are in groups? Just men? Just women? Families? Who socializes in the café? Young? Old? Men? Couples?

12. **Helping a stranger in Mexico**

    This we might be able to do when we are first in Mexico. A situation has to be set up. Stand on a sidewalk studying a map, acting very puzzled and lost. Does anyone come up to you and voluntarily offer assistance? If someone helps: Describe that person; age, sex, other characteristics. Were you able to understand and communicate? If no one helped you do you think that is typical of the Mexican culture? Do you think that someone would help you in the States?

13. **Young people**

    Where do they gather?

    At movies? Cafés? Restaurants? Parks? Other places?

    Do Mexican people around your age seem to have more or less freedom around home than you do? Explain.

14. **Shopping**

    Problems? Abundance, or lack of certain items?

15. **Salesclerks**

    How much time goes by before you are assisted in the store?

    How do you react to the behavior of the Mexican clerk? Does he or she make you nervous or do you appreciate the help?

16. **Newspapers**

    Are there a lot of them? Are they big? Are there foreign papers? City? National? etc.

17. **Graffiti**

    Based on this, what are some concerns of the Mexican people? Do they write the same things as in the States?

    Where do you find graffiti?

18. **People/Machines**

    What is done by people, what by machines? Is this the same in the States?

19. **Postal systems**

    Mail a small package or letter home from the post office.

    Is mailing a package *more* or *less* complicated than in the U.S.?

    What is the rate for mailing an ordinary letter within Mexico? (Mail a letter written in Spanish to one of us while we are there so that we can compare notes as to how long it takes to mail one to yourself and see how long it takes.)

20. **Mexican lottery**

    What is it like?

    How are tickets sold?

    Where are they sold?

21. **Communication and body language**

    (This can be a lot of fun, especially when you start to really notice common traits among the Mexicans and you yourself start to *do* them.)

22. **Architecture, culture, and privacy**

    What are the buildings like? Stores? Dwellings? Businesses? How important is privacy? Why do you say whatever it is that you are saying about privacy?

23. **Bargaining**

    (*regatear*) Observe others—What is it like? Experience it yourself. How do you feel?

Emergencies

Thinking about the worst possible case ahead of time may mean that you'll be able to think more clearly and act more quickly, should the need arise.

Medical emergencies

In a strange city, all the students will be under great physical and emotional stress. If someone falls ill or is injured, don't wait: get medical help right away, not only for that student's sake, but for the sake of the others, who also need your care and attention. Even if the illness or injury turns out not to be serious, getting medical attention immediately will forestall further problems and will also reassure the rest of the group (and, later, the families).

When the students are in their homestays, minor injury or illness may not demand immediate medical attention (see "Watch for fatigue and sickness," Chapter 13). You'll have more time to spend with the student (and with the family who'll be looking after the student) and the student will have more time to rest quietly and let nature take its healing course.

You're ultimately responsible for the students' health, so when in doubt, have the student see a doctor. After all, that's why they all have health insurance. If a student is going to a clinic or to see a doctor, ask her if she'd like you to accompany her. If you don't go, be sure that she takes a health insurance form with her, and go over it with her beforehand so she can get it filled out properly. If you think you *should* go along with her, insist on it.

Losing someone

What if one of the students doesn't show up at the appointed time and place?

Don't leave without him. If the group is scheduled to leave, you may want to let the others go ahead (with another adult, if there is one), but you (or another chaperone) should wait; if necessary, the whole group should wait. Perhaps the student just lost his way or lost track of time; if you are at the meeting place, you'll avoid further confusion and delay as he tries to find the others. When he shows up you can help him rejoin the group. If you're not at the hotel, call there and leave a message for him. Say exactly where you are, and that if the student calls he should either join you or return to the hotel—and stay there. Then call the hotel at intervals to see if he's shown up. When you locate him, you'll have a chance to reassure him or read him the riot act in private.

If the student doesn't show up, you can start tracing him. Wait to do this until you're absolutely sure that he hasn't gone to visit a friend, or fallen asleep at the hotel, or stayed out for a few beers.

Before you go to the police, call your supervisor at school, and describe what's happened. The two of you should decide whether you or she should notify the student's family. The parents and the group must be told what's going on, but chances are that the student will turn up, so it's essential that everyone involved be calm and discreet to avoid alarming the group, the student's family and the community at home.

When you go to the police, take the student's passport number (or his passport, if he didn't have it with him), a photo if you have one, and a description of what he was wearing. Ask the police if there's anything further you can do (e.g., calling the hospitals or the American consulate or embassy) or if you should leave everything in their hands.

While you wait for news, keep the rest of the group occupied. Keeping on the move, seeing and doing new things will help them through their worry, and there's no use in their losing what little time they have in their new surroundings. Do as much with them as possible; they'll need adult leadership and reassurance more than ever. Be as open with them as you discreetly can, but try not to dwell on the problem; taking your mind off it (when you can) will help both you and the students.

Have a good time

Don't forget to enjoy yourself during the city-stay. There will undoubtedly be times when you'll look at the haggard face in the mirror and ask yourself, *"Why* am I doing this?" But don't let yourself get so wound up in the inevitable complications and hassles that you lose sight of the pleasures of the trip. Hang on to your sense of humor, and seek out students who are having a good time—they'll be happy to share their pleasure with you, and it will carry you along. Take time for yourself, too: window-shop, visit museums, take a brisk walk on your own, or sit in a café with a newspaper or your journal. You'll have earned some time to yourself; besides, if you're enjoying yourself, the students will catch your enthusiasm and they'll be happier, too.

13

In the Families

The key to successful homestays is good communication—among all parties: your students, their new families, your counterpart, and yourself. Whatever you can do to open or encourage communication among all these people will make the homestay that much more pleasant for everyone.

Staying healthy

The students will be eating new foods, perhaps on a new schedule; their sleep and rest patterns may change; and their nervousness in their new families may subject their bodies to stress, even though they may not be conscious of its effects.

Encourage the students to eat lightly the first few days, and to drink plenty of fluids. Of course it's especially important for them to take in a lot of liquids in hot climates, but no matter what the climate, drinking fluids and avoiding heavy meals will help the students through their adjustment to the new way of life.

Is tap water safe to drink? You can ask your counterpart about this, but conditions may vary from town to town or even from house to house, depending on the water supply. In general, if the host family offers tap water, it's OK for the students to drink it. If they're in doubt, they can ask for fruit juice, tea, or a soft drink.

Check with students and families within 48 hours

Within the first day or two, you should make a point of talking with each student individually to see how things are going. If the schedule includes a group meeting or outing, try to get there early in order to talk with a few students before the activity starts. Take advantage of lulls in the action (pauses between presentations at a meeting, bus rides on a sightseeing excursion) to circulate among the students. If the group doesn't meet during the first two days, or if you don't have a chance to talk with everyone when it does meet, call the students you missed. Your budget should cover the cost of these calls, whether you call from a public phone or reimburse your host for calls from his phone. The calls can be time-consuming—and, in many countries, expensive—but the students will be glad to hear your voice and if they're having a problem of some kind, you may be able to nip it in the bud; if all is going well, they'll be glad to share their successes. During our first exchange with Switzerland, the group didn't meet for a few days, so I called all the students. Most were doing fine themselves, though several wanted me to know how unhappy one girl was (she'd lost no time sharing her woes with the others). They all spoke English except John, the only boy in the group, whose partner lived in an isolated village outside Geneva. John had had fewer years of French than most of the others, but he greeted me exuberantly:

"Salut, Maggie! Walter est formidable. Je fais de la moto!" and so on, all in French.

Even if there's a problem, adolescents may hesitate to admit anything's wrong: they often feel that if something is wrong, it's probably their fault. Furthermore, asking for help seems like a confession that they're not yet as independent as they'd like to think. If you ask, "How's it going?" they're almost certain to say, "Fine," or at least, "OK, I guess," even though they may feel quite bewildered or frustrated. It's often helpful to ask neutral-sounding questions: paradoxically, questions that ask for factual information are often more likely to uncover students' real feelings than are questions about their feelings. Besides, if there are communication problems between the host family and their student, you may be better able to clarify them if you have facts to go on. For example, if a student says, "I feel left out," it's hard to know where to begin; but if she says, "I try to speak German, but they always speak too fast," and her family says, "We try to speak English to her, but of course we speak German among ourselves," the problem is a little clearer: you can ask the family to speak more slowly, you can ask her to be sure to speak German all the time, and you can ask everyone to keep trying.

Questions to ask the students could include the following:

☐ Does anyone in your family speak English?

☐ Do you usually speak (the host family's language) or English?

☐ What have you been doing?

☐ How much sleep have you been getting?

☐ Do you share a room with someone?

☐ Have you gotten used to the food?

☐ How do you get around? By car, bus, on foot?

☐ What do you have in common with your counterpart?

□ Have you figured out what to do about your laundry? (Months after our return from Geneva, I found that one girl had not washed any of her clothes during our three-week stay: she was too stubborn to ask anyone what she should do, and her host family never asked about it.)

It's also very important to introduce yourself to the host families as soon as possible. Don't wait for them to get in touch with you; they won't, because they'll probably assume either that you're not interested, or that you're too busy to talk with them unless there's a crisis—so you won't hear from them until a small problem has indeed reached crisis proportions. On the other hand, if you take the initiative, so they can see that you want to work with them to make the homestay successful for all concerned, they will confide in you and make it easier for you to keep track of all the students in the group.

Watch for fatigue and sickness

Traveling is tiring; eating new foods is tiring; adapting to a new family's way of life is tiring; and total immersion in a new language is tiring. Both your students and their hosts may need reassurance on this point. The students may misread their fatigue as sickness, and go into a decline, worrying their hosts and the rest of the group; or they may ignore their need for rest, and overexert themselves until they really do fall sick. Host families may misinterpret their guests' natural fatigue for laziness, shyness, or hostility. You can help avoid misunderstanding if you encourage the students to take it easy the first few days; at the same time, explain to their families that they need extra sleep, so the families will understand. The second day of our stay in Switzerland, one of the older students looked a little pale.

"Are you feeling OK?" I asked. She promptly burst into tears.

"I'm just so tired!" she said, weeping helplessly. Fortunately her family was going to the mountains for vacation, and fortunately they were very understanding. When they all arrived at the chalet, she slept for 36 hours, awoke refreshed, and joined the family's activities; everything was fine from then on.

Prolonged fatigue is a common symptom of culture shock; people often retreat into sleep because they feel unable to cope with some aspect of their experience. If a student seems to need inordinate amounts of sleep after the first two or three days, more sleep may not be the solution. You may need to talk seriously with him to see if sleep is his way of refusing to deal with his homestay family, the new language, the group, or homesickness. Often simply talking about such problems helps put them into perspective, so encourage him to bring his feelings out into the open and examine them.

Sometimes fatigue and unfamiliar foods do bring on sickness, often in the form of nausea, stomach cramps, diarrhea, or headache. When this happens, members of the homestay family are likely to get alarmed and upset, feeling that it's somehow their fault. Reassure them and the student: tell them that illness is a common reaction to the stress of travel.

It will be up to you to decide when a student is sick enough to need medical attention. Of course any student who shows signs of acute illness (including fever, diarrhea lasting more than two days, inability to keep down even fluids) should see a doctor. If the student simply has an upset stomach, 24 to 36 hours of bed rest and plenty of fluids (tea or carbonated soft drinks) do wonders. Once when I was visiting friends in a village in Yugoslavia, oily stuffed peppers brought on violent nausea. By morning I was so weak and dizzy that my hosts took me to the nearest clinic, where the doctor prescribed tea and dry toast. Tea and toast! Just what my mother had always given me as a child. Reassured, I immediately began to feel better.

Communication between students and families

I think it's safe to say that most problems between students and their host families stem from unrealistic expectations on one or both sides, or faulty communication, or both. Few students or families are truly inconsiderate. Rather, students expect their families to be warm, welcoming, and solicitous—all the time; while of course at times the families will have to deal with their normal preoccupations: making a living, organizing their family life, and the added responsibility of getting their guests from one place to another and making them feel at home. On the other side, the families expect the students to be adaptable, out-going, and eager to learn—all the time; while at times the students will be tired, confused, bored, homesick, discouraged, or anxious to see their friends.

Of course you and your counterpart will do your best to keep the families and the students from idealizing each other too much ahead of time, but there may still be disappoint-ments on both sides, especially as families compare notes on their guests and students com-pare notes on their families. I feel that in general the students should be the ones to adapt to their families, rather than vice versa. First of all, and practically speaking, the visitors can be much more flexible, because they don't have to bow to the everyday demands of job, school, house and family as their hosts do. Secondly, the students' ostensible purpose in coming is to learn how ordinary families live, and if the families radically change their way of doing things in order to please their guests, the students will come away with a false idea of normal daily life in the new country.

On both sides of our exchanges, students' complaints usually have to do with feeling restricted or isolated:

"My family leaves me at home alone while they work."

"They never go anywhere."

"My partner just works/goes to school/hangs around the house."

"My partner just wants to spend time with his girlfriend/her boyfriend and I feel like a third wheel."

"All my friends are together in town, and I'm stuck in the country with no way to join them."

Not surprisingly, homestay families' comments tend to reflect the other side of the same coin:

"He's on the go every minute."

"She just wants to be with her friends, and they all speak their own language, so our child feels left out."

"He doesn't seem very interested in our family."

"At times, when I'm driving the students around and they're all speaking their own language, I feel like just a chauffeur."

Since every student is unique, as is every family, no two homestay situations will be the same. Better communication could improve most of the situations reflected in the students' and families' comments: if they're aware of their guests' feelings, families may be able to make arrangements so their visitors won't be left home alone; students can make more effort to spend time with their families and show interest in them. Whatever the situation, it isn't likely to improve unless each side knows what the other is feeling, so encourage both parents and students to talk with each other. Don't allow yourself or your counterpart to be drawn into a situation as a go-between: your presence will just muddy the waters. It's fine for either the family or the student, or both, to talk with you; you may be able to suggest some ways to improve the situation, and in any case your sympathetic ear can make the other person feel much better. But above all, encourage the student and the family to talk to each other.

It's a good idea to keep in touch with your counterpart about the problems between a student and his or her family. If your counterpart knows the families well, he may have some useful insights or suggestions to help you deal with the situation. He's as responsible to his students and their families as you are to yours, so if the problem becomes serious, it's only fair that he should have known about it from the start.

Some problems demand a more direct approach. The students may behave in some way that seems harmful to them: they may hitchhike, or hang around places or people that your counterpart or their families have warned against. Some students may miss scheduled meals with their families, or spend their time and attention on other Americans and neglect their families. In these situations the problem isn't so much misunderstanding between families and students as ignorance or willfulness on the students' part. I would hasten to talk privately, directly, and firmly with the students in question, reminding them of their obligations to their host families, their counterparts, and themselves. If they persisted in their offensive behavior, I'd consider sending them home (see "Sending a student home," Chapter 2).

Luckily, easing communication between students and their host families isn't always a matter of solving problems: sometimes it involves passing on compliments from one party to the other. One of our students, whom I'll call Joanne, was rather shy with the other Americans in the group, but she seemed to blossom in her Swiss family. Whenever we ran into her, as we often did because we were on the same bus route, she beamed and told us how nice her family was to her and how much she was enjoying herself. At a pot-luck dinner her Swiss father sought me out to thank me for placing Joanne with them: he couldn't say enough nice things about her. I told him that she was very happy to be with them, which pleased him, and the next day, when I told her how much her family liked her, she was overwhelmed. She'd obviously thought that the family's warmth had nothing to do with *her;* she needed an outsider to let her know that they welcomed her not only because they were kind, hospitable people, but because she was a wonderful guest.

Help the students show gratitude

Though this chapter has concentrated on potential problems and how to avoid or resolve them, most of your students' homestays will probably be like Joanne's: most students get along fine with their families and have a wonderful time. You can suggest ways for them to show gratitude to all the people who made the whole experience possible.

The group can return their host families' hospitality, at least in some small measure, by inviting the families to a get-together at the end of their homestay. Your counterpart may have to help the group find a suitable location (a school cafeteria or fraternal club's hall would be suitable; the room needn't be formal), and you may need to ask to use some families' kitchens, but after that the students should take over. If recipes and ingredients are available, the families would probably enjoy eating some American dishes prepared by the students. In addition to the food, which can be served as a sit-down meal (with the students serving) or buffet-style, some entertainment might relax and interest the families. The entertainment needn't be long: students could sing a few songs (preferably some in English and some in the hosts' language) and perhaps teach everyone an American song; or students could present skits (in the hosts' language) about their stay, or show slides of your community in the U.S.

Finally, the party can be the occasion for the students to thank their families publicly for their hospitality. To mark the occasion, each student can give his or her family some small gift. To avoid embarrassment at this public event, all the presents should be similar (though not necessarily identical). They could be either something the students have brought from home specifically for this occasion (see "Presents for the homestay families," Chapter 10), or a customary gift in the host country (flowers or candy, or both, are usually appropriate in Western European countries). If there's something left in the group's emergency fund, you can distribute some money from it to each student for this present. One special gift is probably also in order: a present from you and your group will show your gratitude for all the unsung labor your counterpart has done for the students.

Don't forget the folks back home: someone should write on behalf of the whole group to the people at school and in the community who helped them on their way, to let them know what a good time the group is having. That someone needn't be you. Ask all the students to whom they think the group should write; then ask for volunteers to write postcards, which will be particularly welcome coming from the students.

Enjoy yourself

During the homestay you have a lot of responsibilities: taking part in the group's activities, keeping up with individual students, and dealing with your own counterpart and/or host family. Furthermore, we teachers often feel tremendous pressure not to waste a single opportunity to see new sights or to gather information and materials.

At the same time, it's important to build up your energy reserves. Take time out whenever you can, and be good to yourself. Take a walk—or a nap; go to the movies; take a little excursion by bus or train (or even by rented car!) for a half-day or a day—even a couple of days if there's another leader to share your responsibilities. Making some time for yourself and making yourself relax will help you maintain your perspective and your sense of humor—and will help everyone in the long run.

14

Back Home

Students should write to their host families right away

Politeness demands that the students write to their host families *immediately* upon their return—to let their families know they returned safely, and of course to thank them again for their hospitality. Once home, the students may get so caught up in their own families, their friends, and their schoolwork that they put off writing until it becomes a stale formality; try to prevent this from happening. While the group is still together on the way back home, explain to the students how important it is to write to their host families. Tell them that you'll be following up to make sure they've done it—and then follow up. Within a day or two of our return, I distributed a short form to each student:

I have mailed a letter to my homestay family to thank them.

_____(date)   _____(name)

Most wrote in the burst of enthusiasm that followed their return, and turned in their forms within a week. A few stragglers managed to put off writing for nearly a month, but without pressure from other students and me, who knows how long they'd have taken to write?

Help students give a good impression
of the trip

When the students return to school, you'll probably find that other students immediately find out about whatever went wrong: that Tim abandoned his stay-at-home girlfriend for Susie, that Jack got drunk, that Ann got heavily involved with her counterpart's brother— or even that you lost your temper and yelled at the group for 10 minutes right in public in front of the Prado. Students will naturally spread bad news: it's dramatic, it makes them look good by contrast, and it's easily told. All their own experience is so complex that they'll be hard-pressed to understand it themselves, much less sum it up for everyone who asks, "So how was the trip?"

Though you can ask the students to be discreet when they talk about the trip, there's no use trying to suppress gossip, no matter how distasteful you find it. Trying to suppress it will only give it added urgency and appeal: "Mr. Jones said we weren't supposed to tell *any-one,* but . . . " Instead, encourage them to think about—and tell—the best and worst things that happened to them personally.

The group should thank people
who helped out

Individuals and organizations who helped the students will appreciate a brief note thanking them for their support. The notes can be written any time after your return, though the students will be more willing if you don't wait too long.

Ask for a few volunteers to write on behalf of the whole group. A note-writing party makes less work for everyone, since you can have all the necessary materials on hand, and the writers can agree on a general form for the letters, which can then be adapted for each recipient. The group can draw up a list of people and organizations to be thanked. The list should include individuals (e.g., your counterpart, particularly supportive administrators or public figures in either country, merchants who donated goods and services) and organizations or companies—both local ones that supported the group in some way, and places the group visited in the host country. If the tour was purely commercial, of course there's no need for a thank-you note, but often your group will have received a special welcome in places that don't ordinarily accept student groups, and the people who welcomed you will appreciate your gratitude.

Because so few groups bother to thank their benefactors in writing, your group's letter will be particularly memorable. In a small town like Brattleboro, merchants and companies are besieged by student groups asking for contributions of all kinds. A representative of one of the larger companies told Skip Gordon, head of our exchange's coordinating committee, that our note was the first written thank-you that that company had ever received.

Letdown and how to combat it

After the euphoria of coming home to their families and friends, distributing presents, showing off their own souvenirs, and talking about the highlights of the trip, students will probably feel tremendous letdown, which is as natural a stage in a trip as culture shock.

After their two or three weeks away, the students feel different, and in many ways they are different: they've discovered new things about themselves and the world, and many of them have gained vast amounts of self-confidence and independence. At the same time, the family and friends they left behind haven't changed perceptibly, and don't fully understand how the travelers have changed.

One way that students can minimize their sense of letdown is to find outlets for their enthusiasm among groups of people who would like to hear about their travels: oddly, casual acquaintances or complete strangers are often more interested in the details of the trip than family or close friends are. These audiences can be outside the school (see "Talk shows" and "Take the show on the road," Chapter 7), but there may also be interested groups within the school system. Some teachers will require students to give presentations to a class as part of their assignment for that class, but other teachers might also welcome your students' sharing their experience with a class—which need not be the students' own. Younger students are especially appreciative audiences, and their enthusiasm makes the high school students feel good; at the same time, a presentation about the trip may inspire the younger ones to travel, and even to take the courses they'll need to qualify them for such a trip when they reach the appropriate age.

Some students can arrange these presentations on their own, but a letter from you to your colleagues, perhaps with a brief signup form they can fill in and send back if they're interested, might also generate some invitations.

Encourage the students to take along some visual aids: a map, a *few* of their pictures (or some postcards or commercial slides, if their own pictures aren't available), brochures and souvenirs from places they visited.

Pete, who had drunk wine to such excess in Paris, talked to his English class a few days after our return from Switzerland and invited me to the presentation. The class was rowdy, and Pete was no Goody Two-Shoes himself. He wasn't used to speaking in public, and he was visibly nervous as he stood facing the class. He began with the flight to Paris.

"It was so neat," he said. "We were 35,000 feet up, way above the clouds. We flew over Nova Scotia, and we were having dinner on the plane while everybody down on earth was sleeping." He talked about our visit to Red Cross headquarters in Geneva, and the Red Cross's work tracing refugees; he described the sleek new Rolex factory, with its tinted glass and filtered air, and passed around glossy Rolex brochures. The students were quiet, hanging on every sentence.

Finally he ran down, and said, "Well, I guess that's it. Does anybody have any questions?"

"Yeah," said one of the boys in the front row. "How was the beer in Switzerland?"

"I didn't drink it," said Pete. A ripple of disbelieving laughter ran through the room.

"I drank a little too much in Paris," he said, trying to explain, "and I got pretty sick, so I didn't drink at all in Switzerland."

"Jeez!" "Chicken!" Disgusted murmurs from the rest of the class.

Pete held his ground.

"Well, some of the other kids in the group drank—a lot—and they had some problems, so . . . . " His voice trailed off, and he shrugged. It was too hard to explain to them how he'd changed; he was just—*different* now.

15

The American Side of an Exchange

Families should plan their guests' activities

Though it's up to you (working with your counterpart) to organize the trip abroad, it's the families who should take the responsibility for organizing the foreign students' stay in your community. First of all, if the families plan their guests' schedule, they'll have a personal stake in the program and will take care to prepare the students for each activity. If you alone planned the program, many families would remain passive, delivering their guests to the appointed meeting place at the appointed time, and otherwise leaving it all in your hands. Furthermore, when the families get together to plan the visitors' stay, they have contacts and resources in the community beyond any one person's reach. Their friends, neighbors, relatives, and co-workers will lend equipment, donate goods and services, and welcome the students in a variety of ways.

It's important that all the families do their share and feel involved. Of course some families will do more than others. If you wish, you can try to regulate each family's share in the work; I prefer to rely on direct requests for help to families who haven't done so much, peer pressure from other families, lots of appreciation for the families who take on more than their share of the work, and the knowledge that those families are getting more out of the exchange than the others.

All of this is not to say that your own ideas and suggestions shouldn't receive consideration. You do represent the school, and you know the foreign students' backgrounds and expectations better than any of the other adults.

Brainstorm with the families:
some suggestions

Once you know the dates of the students' visit, meet with all the families to get ideas for the visitors' program. Ask for everyone's ideas of what the visitors should see and do; someone should write down all the suggestions on a blackboard (or large piece of paper taped to a wall) so everyone can see them.

Here are some possible activities:

- a reception to welcome the visitors to the community. Community and school officials could speak to the students. It's important to have some entertainment or something to do, so people don't just stand around: one year we had a square-dance, which turned out to be a great way to mix people of different ages. One or two people recruited families to bring food;

- sightseeing that reflects differences of climate, geography, or culture: for urban students visiting the country, visits to a farm or a small airport; for rural students visiting the city, cultural events (opera, ballet, theater), or visits to landmarks. For both, museums or historical sites; tours of industries that manufacture products from raw materials. It doesn't matter whether the finished products are chocolates, pencils, books, watches, maple candies, or bottles of wine—the fascination is in seeing the steps involved in making everyday products that we take for granted;

- outings with families. These have been among the most successful activities on both sides of our exchanges, because people are more at ease when they're *doing* things together, and groups can form and dissolve informally in the course of the activity. Some possible outings are:

  - a cross-country ski tour, with picnics;

  - a hike, with picnics;

  - a skating party and then cocoa at someone's house;

  - a bike ride;

  - a swimming party;

  - a hayride;

  - bowling;

  - a trip to an amusement-park or fair;

  - spectator sports—but *only* if guests are already familiar with the game; otherwise, even if the hosts are glad to explain the rules, the game probably won't hold the guests' attention very long, as we found when we took the Swiss to a Red Sox game in Boston;

  - cookouts, clambakes, barbecues, etc., especially if everybody has to pitch in to fix the food;

  - seasonal events: trick-or-treating at Halloween, Christmas caroling, working on a Fourth of July float. For example, the Swiss students in our second exchange arrived just in time to put the finishing touches on our group's Fourth of July float. Sponsored by the Windham County Dairy Council, the float featured a live calf; one hill made of chicken-wire and green paper napkins, topped by an American flag; another, somewhat steeper hill, made of chicken-wire and white paper napkins, with a Swiss flag at the top; tying it all together, a banner proclaiming, "FROM THE SWISS ALPS TO THE GREEN MOUNTAINS, MILK IS A NATURAL—B.U.H.S. SWISS EXCHANGE;" and 60 exuberant Swiss and American students waving to the onlookers and passing out "Milk drinkers make better lovers" bumper stickers.

● a scavenger hunt, which makes the visitors use their English to get information about some aspects of the community they might not have seen otherwise. A sample follows:

1. Go to the Serendipity ice-cream parlor. Explain in English: what are "jimmies"? _____

   _____

2. What two flags are flying on the outside of Baker's Bookstore?

   _____

3. What's one of the films coming soon to the Paramount?

   _____

4. What's one of today's specials at the Autumn Winds?

   _____

5. What was the original function of the Brooks House building?

   _____

6. Ask for a parking ticket from the police headquarters.

7. Who was the sculptor of the statue "The Snow Angel" in the library?

   _____

8. Ask for an "I LOVERMONT" bumper sticker at the Chamber of Commerce.

9. For what war is there a memorial on the Common? _____

10. What was the original function of the Municipal Building? _____

11. What's the charitable activity of the Shriners' organization?

12. How much is a plate of manicotti at the Via Condotti?

13. What's the price of an egg slicer at Brown and Roberts hardware store?

   _____

● a farewell party for the guests. We've organized pot-luck suppers, followed by dancing or a folk concert, but the format will depend on your community and your budget. People in the community who have been very involved with the exchange might appreciate an invitation to this party.

At this first meeting, the families can also discuss the budget for the visit, at least in a general way: do they want to raise money as a group to cover at least some of the expenses of the guests' visit, or do they prefer that each family be assessed for its share of the budget?

Set up committees

Committees work more efficiently than big groups, so at the first meeting you might suggest that volunteers, both students and parents, form a committee to organize the visit and report back to the whole group with a tentative schedule and a budget. If the families decided to raise money as a group, a separate committee could set up and coordinate the fund–raising efforts (see Chapter 8 for fund–raising ideas).

Both committees will need all the time they can get. The coordinating committee needs time to meet, make phone calls, wait for the calls to be returned, draw up a budget, order tickets, reserve halls, charter buses, present their schedule to the whole group, change the schedule, and send the final version to the foreign guests. Fund raising also takes a great deal of time, so both groups should start work as soon as possible.

You can work more or less closely with either or both of these committees. Encourage the group organizing the visit to maintain variety and a balance between activities that are pure entertainment and those that will inform the students. The American students may lean toward entertainment. Our group wrangled about whether to take our visitors to the Shelburne Museum collection of Americana or to Boston to shop. Several of the students said confidently that *they'd* rather go to Boston, so they were sure the Swiss would, too. Finally we compromised, planning one trip to Boston and a second, shorter one to the Sturbridge Village museum. Later, in Geneva, after our hosts had arranged for Alpenhorn players to play for us and a flag-thrower to demonstrate his skill, one of the students turned to me and said, "That was neat. Remember when we talked about going to the museum or to Boston? I said we should go to Boston, but now I kind of see why they might like the museum. A lot of the stuff we think is just normal would all be new to them."

Prepare families for the homestay

For many of the families, the foreign students will be the first houseguests to stay so long—or at least the first long-term houseguests who aren't also members of the family. The families may have difficulty sorting out their responsibilities and their expectations, and living up to them. Unfortunately, often they're unaware of the potential difficulty before the students arrive, so they may see no need to discuss curfews, driving, and other questions that can take on urgent importance during the visit. Even if the families do talk over some of these questions, they can't anticipate every problem, but if they don't talk them over at all, they'll feel not only unprepared, but also isolated: each family will wonder what's wrong with it (or its student) rather than realizing that complications naturally arise between a family and its guest.

The first set of questions addresses parents and their responsibilities; at the same time, it is useful for both parents and students to talk over these situations. Discussion can be most productive in small groups, each consisting of some adults and some students—but not from the same family. In this way the generations can express themselves freely. You can simply distribute a copy of the questions to each group; someone (preferably a student) can take on the task of recording the group's comments on each questions. Then, when all the small groups have discussed each question, the entire group can compare their reactions.

The point of the questions is not so much to reach any conclusions as to stimulate thought and communication—and therefore confidence—within each family and among all the host families in the group. Parents' responsibilities for their guests are naturally different from their children's responsibilities. Adolescents would often prefer to ignore unpleasant possibilities until those possibilities have become harsh reality, while parents are more likely to want to confront potential problems before they have a chance to be realized.

How Will You Handle It?

1. Your guest likes to sleep late in the morning; your family always gets up early (or perhaps your guest likes to go to bed very early and your family stays up late.)

2. You insist that your own children only ride with people you know are good drivers. Your guest announces that he's going to the beach, and when you ask who's driving, he says he's not sure.

3. It's your five-year-old daughter's birthday, and the family always celebrates birthdays with a special dinner and a cake, and then goes out for ice cream. Just before you sit down to dinner, your guest calls to say that she's staying in town for pizza.

4. One of the Americans is having a party. Your son isn't feeling well, but your guest is very anxious to go, so you take him, telling him that if he needs a ride home, he should call. At midnight you go to bed. Your son says his counterpart came in at 4:00 (Alternative: at 2:30 the phone rings and your guests asks you to come pick him up).

5. Your guest asks to use the phone each time she wants to make a call: finally you tell her she doesn't need to ask, because the phone isn't very expensive. One evening you hear her speaking her own language, and your daughter says the visitor has called her own family, without reversing the charges.

6. Your guest has fallen in love, and spends every spare moment with the object of his or her affections. Your own child is beginning to feel left out; besides, the couple is rapidly becoming very intimate in public, embarrasing the other students.

7. Your guest is polite, but she's never hungry at mealtimes.

8. Your own child seems to be a different person. Normally fairly conscientious about his schoolwork and his responsibilities around the house, now he wants to be on the go every minute. He wants to go out every night, schoolnight or weekend, and when he's not out, there's a noisy group of young people at your house. "Aw, come on," he says "We want to have fun while our guests are here."

9. Your child and your guest seem totally indifferent to each other, or even seem to dislike each other.

The following questions, written from the foreign student's point of view, helped our *students* focus on problems their guests might have here, so we discussed them at a meeting for students only—and then sent copies home for parents to see. You may prefer to have parents discuss them at a group meeting. You may also wish to change the questions to reflect the particular culture you're dealing with.

The students can discuss these questions as they did the others, in small groups. One student in each group can read the questions one by one while another student records the others' comments. Then the whole group can come back together to talk over their comments.

If the Americans have already gone abroad, they will probably recognize some of the situations in reverse: for example, our students noticed that their Swiss counterparts' families ate together much more often than their own families did. On the other hand, if the Americans have not yet gone abroad, they may need some guidance in putting themselves in their guests' place: for instance, they may say that their counterparts should not need help in understanding English. The Americans may need to be reminded that when they are abroad, everything will seem confusing and new for the first few days and they will welcome their counterparts' help.

After students have talked over their reactions to the questions, they can explore them further by acting them out. Each small group can choose a particular question to role-play, or the groups can draw a questions at random.

Questions for discussion

1. My family talks so fast and slurs their words so much that we have difficulty understanding each other. When I don't understand something, they shout at me. My counterpart doesn't explain anything to me in French. What should I do?

2. The family has the TV or radio on almost all the time, even when they talk to me or each other. It's hard for me to understand them with the background noise.

3. My family doesn't seem close at all: they hardly ever eat meals together, and even when they do, they don't talk about what they've been doing. Do they really like each other?

4. A lot of people come into my family's home. I don't even know who they all are. What should I do? Should I introduce myself? Also, when people greet me they ask, "How are you?" but they never seem to listen to my answer. What am I supposed to say?

5. Americans seem to have so many *things*. There are piles of old newspapers in the garage; there are lots of books and magazines in the house that no one seems to read, and I even see old cars in people's yards. Why do Americans save so many old things?

6. I have only a few changes of clothes, but the Americans change their clothes several times each day. Do they think we Swiss don't dress well?

7. My counterpart drinks milk or sweet drinks all the time. There is never mineral water or wine with dinner—but some of the Americans talk a lot about getting drunk. How can I find out what is acceptable?

8. During the day, my counterpart doesn't sit down for meals—we just eat some snacks very rapidly. Why are Americans in such a hurry?

9. When my counterpart is working, I'm not sure what I'm supposed to be doing.

10. My family drives everywhere, even when it would be easier to walk. I need exercise, but I don't want to offend them. What should I do?

If the students will visit school,
prepare both school and visitors

Preparation will make the students' visit to your school smoother for everyone—not least for you, as you try to carry on with your normal teaching at the same time.

How much time the visitors spend at school will depend on the rest of their schedule. If they'll spend more than a day there, they'll need a clearcut idea of where they're supposed to be and what they're supposed to be doing; otherwise they'll be tempted to wander around the school, congregate in the halls or the cafeteria, or leave school to go shopping.

Enlist your counterpart's help in planning this part of the visit. If you can find a place for them to meet, does your counterpart wish to gather the whole group together at specific times? They could use the time to talk over their experiences in their families or to learn English: perhaps you can arrange to have your counterpart or some of your colleagues cover your classes while you help the visitors with their English; or perhaps one of those colleagues could help them. They could also learn about the American way of life. Other teachers, some students, or speakers from outside the school could talk with the group about specific aspects of American society and culture: sports, politics, history, geography, the role of TV, jazz, folk music, and so on.

A second way to occupy the students is to schedule them into classes in advance. You can send your counterpart some copies of the school's course listings; vocational or other courses that aren't familiar to the guests might especially interest them. If the course descriptions are hard for outsiders to understand, send an explanation along with them. The students can then indicate which courses they'd like to see, and, taking their preferences into account, you and your students can arrange an individual schedule for each visitor, as if he or she were enrolling at the school. The school's guidance office might even be willing to help you arrange the schedules. Then when the visitors arrive, their hosts can help them find their way around.

If it's impractical to work out an individual schedule for each visitor, the visitors can simply follow their hosts' schedules. Both hosts and teacher should make a special effort to make the visitors feel welcome: hosts should introduce their guests to their teachers, and teachers should then allow time for the hosts to introduce their guests to the rest of the class.

As you can see, teachers play a large role in welcoming the foreign students to the school. Simply giving over a few minutes of class time to talking with the visitors can help a lot. Teachers can ask whether that particular course is taught in the visitor's home school; how it's taught; how it fits into the general curriculum. In some classes, the teacher can actually use the students as resources: visitors can talk about their region's geography, history, or political system in social studies classes, or they can give new realism to role plays in foreign language classes.

If the visitors will be in school for several days without prearranged schedules, their hosts should help them attend classes that particularly interest them. Depending on how strict your school is, the students may be able to arrange this themselves, simply by asking the teachers' permission. If more formality is required, you or the guidance office or a sympathetic administrator could help with the red tape. At Montpelier High School, Swiss students spent two days with home economics students. The first day, the visitors talked about Swiss food with the class. The following day, the Americans cooked for their guests—with the guests' help.

The visitors will feel especially at ease in the school if they prepare projects that they can present to classes. The projects can be about almost any aspect of their country or region (see "Help students develop projects," Chapter 6). You can then distribute a list of visitors and their projects to your colleagues, who can indicate which ones they'd like their classes to see.

In order to enlist the faculty's support, give teachers the information they need well ahead of time. Let them know when the visitors will be at school and what they'll be doing, and update the information as it becomes more specific.

The visitors, too, should know before they come what to expect—and what's expected of them. Keep your counterpart abreast of the plans, and through him, let the students know what they'll be doing and what the school will ask of them: for example, adherence to rules about class attendance, passes, where they may or may not eat and smoke.

When the guests arrive at school, arrange for a tour of the school, with introductions to people the visitors should know: the principal, the librarian, secretaries and cafeteria workers who work closely with students.

Distribute a schedule of the visitors' activities

When the students and their families agree on a program of activities for the visitors and all the details are set, everyone involved with the exchange should get a copy of the schedule. It can be quite informal, and you should print up plenty of copies for families, visitors, chaperones, and school officials. You may want to post a copy in the teachers' room or even distribute copies to teachers; the schedule can be the basis for a newspaper article or a local news story on the radio.

The schedule should contain the following information for each activity:

- a meeting place and time;
- the name of the person in charge;
- whether the activity is optional or required;
- how much money the students should bring, if any;
- arrangements for meals: whether students should bring a bag lunch;
- what special clothes or equipment the students will need, if any;
- when and where the activity will end;
- a rain date.

The group may have already printed a more formal program to serve as a fund-raising device or as part of your public relations campaign (see "Sell ads for a program," Chapter 8, and "Print up material," Chapter 7). This final schedule should supplement rather than replace the formal program. There's no need for advertisers or benefactors to know that on Tuesday everyone should bring a bag lunch, a swimsuit, and 75¢ to the pool. All those details would dilute the advertising or the message of thanks.

Keep your sense of humor

When the train, the plane, or the bus arrives, take a deep breath, smile, and take another deep breath. Whether or not the guests' leader is staying with you during their visit, he or she will probably depend on you to interpret the host families' actions or attitudes.

"Ana's family watches so much TV!" the leader may say. "She says it's on all day, and they don't talk to her much."

"Pedro's counterpart likes to drive everywhere. Pedro says he'd rather walk or bicycle sometimes, but his family discourages him."

The families may also call on you to interpret their guests' actions or attitudes or to advise them on their responsibilities.

"Should I let him go to an all-night party? We wouldn't let our own child go."

"Her clothes are really—well—indecent. They're so tight! Should I say anything? I don't want to hurt her feelings, but people will get the wrong idea."

"He doesn't seem very interested in us. He hardly ever smiles. Are we doing something wrong?"

"She put my best frying pan in the oven and melted the handle. Should I let her pay for it?"

As when you're abroad with your own students, don't feel that you must solve all these problems yourself. You can't. You can listen, you can soothe or reassure, you can encourage families to communicate with their guests and vice versa; you can share problems with your counterpart and, if decisions have to be made, make them with him. Above all, you can keep taking deep breaths, and you can keep smiling.

Fortunately, it's not always hard to keep smiling. The presence of a foreign guest sometimes makes families look at themselves in a new way that can be very rewarding in the end.

"We've had a ball," one mother told me. "She's so open and friendly. The other day she said, 'You don't eat together very often, do you?' I just didn't know what to say, but you know, she was right. Jerry gets home late from work, and usually by that time the kids have eaten and gone off somewhere. I'd never really thought about it until she mentioned it—but she's shown us a lot about our own family!"

It's easy to maintain your sense of humor if the people you deal with are as cheerful as that mother—or another who told me that her Swiss visitor and another Swiss girl had been dancing in front of an upstairs window. This mother had had no objection to her guests' choice of music, but she'd been horrified to learn that they were dancing in the nude. Still, she was laughing as she told me about it.

Hosting foreign counterparts can be as educational for American students as traveling. They learn about their own culture as it's reflected in their visitors' reactions to it, and a few will understand their parents much better after the visit. One student found herself caught between her guest and her parents.

"I have to explain my family's rules and our way of doing things to her," Carla said. "I don't like it. Now I know what my parents go through, because even though their rules are perfectly reasonable, it's a drag having to enforce them. I'm used to being the enforcee, not the enforcer." Eventually Carla's parents and her guest were able to talk directly with each other; in the meantime Carla walked a few kilometers in her parents' shoes.

Thank everybody—in writing

When the guests have left (amid more tears than you ever imagine possible), letters of thanks should go to everyone who helped with the exchange. Wait until the families have had a chance to resume their daily lives, but not longer than two or three weeks after the visit. For details on how to organize writing these thank-you notes, see "The group should thank people who helped out" in Chapter 14.

16

Credit and Evaluation

If you and the students plan the trip with care, prepare for it thoroughly, and throw your-selves into it, you will all learn vast amounts, and there's no reason for students not to get academic credit for what they learn. Mention of the trip will enhance your students' tran-scripts, showing college admissions officers that the students' interest in foreign language—or social studies or drama or whatever the trip's focus was—goes beyond the standard classroom offerings. Academic credit can affect the students' attitude, too: when the trip is part of school (albeit far more amusing than most schoolwork), it's more serious than a mere vacation. If the students don't seem to be taking the trip seriously enough, you can remind them of their academic obligations. They're more likely to feel responsible to you as a representative of the school, especially if you can grant or withhold credit, than to you as an individual adult, no matter how much they may like and respect you.

You'll have to decide well ahead of time on the criteria for granting credit. Your school may have very specific rules governing academic credit, and it may be impossible to make the trip fit those rules. If so, look into the possibility of other sorts of credit: for example, some of our students who didn't want academic credit used the trip for extracurricular points toward admission to National Honor Society.

Since our students would be spending nearly three weeks with French-speaking fami-lies, we in the language department thought that their French would inevitably improve, particularly their spoken French and listening comprehension. In our written presentation to the school board requesting credit for the students, we noted in some detail both what we expected the students to learn and which specific experiences would help them learn it. The program M. Troesch had sent helped us enormously in preparing this presentation. We went on to describe the orientation the students were undergoing, the projects they were working on, and our plans for evaluating what they would learn.

The school board accepted our three rather informal criteria for credit: "successful completion of the trip," which I determined; a journal, which each student had to complete and turn in (with the understanding that I wouldn't read any pages that were covered or clipped together); and completion of a long self-evaluation, which each student turned in after the trip.

You may wish to measure your students' progress in a more formal way, or the school may require a more formal evaluation. Below are some possible ways to evaluate what students learn, but first you must think about just what it is that you're evaluating.

What do you want to evaluate?
How will you go about it?

Is there certain objective information you hope the students will learn during the trip? Do you want them to know specific facts about the plays the group will see, the places it will visit, the history of the host country?

Do you expect all the students to attain a certain objective competency in the foreign language by the time they return? Should they all have mastered a certain number of tenses of a given list of verbs? Must they all learn certain phrases or idiomatic expressions?

Perhaps your goals are less clearly defined. Do you want each student simply to know *more* about the host country than he or she knew before the trip? Do you want the students to understand and speak the language more easily and confidently? Do you want them to be more aware of their own country and culture?

Whatever your goals for the students, it's important to fit your evaluation to what you expect them to learn. If the students travel together during the whole trip, see the same sights, and spend most of their free time together, it can be fair to test the whole group on specific information they learned during the trip. On the other hand, the students may start the trip with different language skills and knowledge of the culture, and then spend most of their time abroad in homestays; it would hardly be fair to test all these students on the same specific information, since they'll all learn different things from their families.

Whether you're measuring language learning, cultural knowledge, or factual information, keep your questions practical. For example, language students may not greatly enlarge their knowledge of the other language's grammatical structure or even their active vocabulary. Therefore many standard language tests will only disappoint and frustrate your students. Most of those tests are designed to evaluate "classroom" learning, with its goals of good grammar and specific vocabulary, whereas the students will have learned to communicate through sentence fragments, gestures, and slang. Only an evaluation that measures this real communication will accurately reflect what the students actually learned. The individual interview described in Chapter 6, administered before and after the trip, is one way to evaluate the students' ability to communicate in another language.

Much more dramatic than improved vocabulary or grammar will be the improvement in the students' comprehension and confidence. Especially after having been immersed in the language during a homestay—and having survived, and enjoyed it—most of the students will feel much more positive and confident about the language. Some will realize for the first time that the language isn't just a course in school, but a means of communicating their most essential needs and feelings. After we'd been abroad for two weeks, one student voiced this change in attitude.

"You know what, Mrs. Cassidy?" he said in a confidential tone. "Of course I'm used to it now, but when we first got here I kept wondering when my family was going to start speaking English. I was kind of surprised when they kept speaking French all the time. But now it seems *natural* to speak French."

Though social scientists might disagree, I think it's impossible—and unnecessary—to quantify this sort of development in a student's attitude toward a new language or culture. Still, I think it's very important that the students themselves think about what they've learned.

The journal

I'm certain that only a few of our students would have kept journals had they not been a requirement for credit, but as it was, almost all the students did. The journals ranged from sketchy collages of ticket stubs, menus, and candy wrappers, through episodic stream-of-consciousness writing, to volumes of minutely detailed observations about the students' surroundings, their new families, and their reaction to both. One girl kept hers faithfully in French.

It was fairly easy to evaluate how much effort had gone into each journal. They didn't always contain the whole truth: knowing that I'd read them (and wishing, perhaps, to share them with their families), most students left out the details of their racier adventures. I found out long afterward that one girl had gone the other way: she'd made up some of the dramatic events in her journal.

A few students, making only minimal efforts to document their trip, were content to glue in souvenirs and label them: "My lift ticket at Zermatt," or "A brochure from the museum." Even these collections of objects at least partly fulfilled the journals' purpose, which was to take the students outside their experience and make them organize it in some way and reflect on it. Most of the students went much further, providing narration to accompany their souvenirs. Even journals that started out as travelogues of the "First-we-went-to-Notre-Dame.-Then-we-went-to-Montmartre" variety soon began to reflect the students' individual enthusiasms. Because they were so caught up in their experience, the students wrote unself-consciously, and their voices come clearly across the page to the reader. Jenny wrote:

> We had an easy landing, however. The airport was huge, with round cement buildings w/ a lot of glass. There was a separate building for each branch of airplane. After waiting 45 minutes in the airport to gather luggage, find a bus and move our tons of luggage into the bus. It was really crowded and we had to sit on boards that came from one seat to another. They were pretty comfortable.

Informal self-evaluation

As I wasn't under pressure to produce statistical evidence of my students' progress, I drew up a questionnaire covering every aspect of the trip. The students' answers helped me evaluate what each student learned; they showed me the program's strengths and weaknesses, so that I'd know how to improve it for another group; above all, I hoped the questions would make the students reflect on their experience in a new way.

The questionnaire follows; you'll see that there are neither right nor wrong answers. I tried to make the questions specific enough to focus the students' thinking and open-ended enough so they could answer as fully as they wished.

Note: the grade each student gave himself or herself at the end of the questionnaire heavily influenced but didn't determine the grade the student received. When I gave a different grade, I explained my reasons for changing it.

SELF-EVALUATION—INFORMAL

Vermont—Genève

février-mars 1981

Evaluation individuelle

Nom: _____

    This evaluation serves two purposes: it is a self-evaluation for you and at the same time a tool for us to evaluate the exchange itself. Please answer each question as honestly and as completely as you can. You will probably find that you will get as much out of the evaluation as you put into it. Please continue on the other side if you need room.

I. Before departure

Why did you decide to take part in the exchange?

What did you hope to accomplish or get out of it?

Did you learn about Switzerland itself during orientation?

If so, *what* did you learn?

What do you *wish* you'd learned about Switzerland before you got there?

What was the most useful about the orientation session?

What was least useful to you about them?

Did you get to know new people in the group before we left?

How seriously did you take the orientation sessions?

Fund raising: do you feel the group did enough? Too much?

      How much of the total cost of the trip ($800 + spending money) did *you personally* contribute (as opposed to parents, grandparents, etc.)? _____

      Did you have enough money?

Please list the fund-raising activities you participated in:

Please list what you can remember we did during orientation sessions (that you didn't mention as most/least useful):

Did you feel that communication within the group was OK, that you generally knew what was going on? If not, please give examples:

Did you learn any useful French before we left? If yes, *what?*

What French would you like to have learned that you didn't?

How many cards/letters/packages did you send to your Swiss counterpart or family before our arrival? About _____

How many cards/letters/packages did you get? About _____

Was the dinner at the Cassidy's worthwhile?

> If so, why?

> If not, how could it have been better?

Was the luggage hike worthwhile?

> If so, why?

> If not, how could it have been better?

Did you feel that you understood the purpose of the presentations that you were asked to do?

How did you prepare your project?

How much time did you spend preparing it? About _____ hours

Did you feel adequately *prepared* for Paris in the following areas; if not, please describe what you'd have liked as preparation:

> getting around

> the hotel

> things to do and see

II. Through Paris

Transportation from BUHS to the hotel (bus to Boston; plane; bus; métro)—do you have any suggestions for improvements?

Hotel: what comments or suggestions do you have?

> location

> facilities

> personnel

> (other)

Did you have enough time on your own in Paris? Too much?

What was the very first thing you noticed about Paris?

Where did you eat in Paris?   *What* did you eat?

1st day	_____	lunch	_____
	_____	supper	_____
2nd day	_____	lunch	_____
	_____	supper	_____

What sites did you visit?

1.   5.

2.   6.

3.   7.

4.   8.

What do you especially want to see or do the most the next time you visit Paris?

In what situations did you speak French?

What is your favorite memory of Paris?

How did you find the French people you met? Give examples.

How would you describe the evening at Deirdre Baker's?

What other activities would you suggest—for the entire group—in the evening?

What would you have done the second evening if you hadn't had to stay with the whole group? (Please be more specific than "go out.")

III. Homestay

What foods did you eat that you'd never eaten?

What new food did you like best?

Which one did you like least?

Did you feel that you had to eat things you didn't want to? Why or why not?

Attitudes:

Can you describe your Swiss family's attitude toward the following things? Be as specific as you can, then put a *D* in front of the item if their attitude was different from what you were used to. Put an *S* if their attitude was the same as yours.

_____ Cars

_____ Phones

_____ Food

_____ Clothes

_____ Family

_____ Speaking other languages

_____ Honesty

_____ Patriotism

_____ Work

_____ TV

_____ Sports

_____ School/education

_____ Cleanliness

_____ Politics

_____ the USA

Language:

What percentage of the time did you speak French with your Swiss family? About _____%

Please list and describe situations *outside* the family in which you spoke French.

     1.

     2.

     3.

     4.

     5.

     (continue on back if necessary)

Of these (including family situations) which were the hardest to deal with in French? Why?

Did you reach a point when you began to feel comfortable speaking French?   Describe.

Did you learn as much French as you'd expected?

What French did you learn that you hadn't expected?

What would you have liked to learn that you didn't?

How did you measure your progress?

When only the Americans were together, did you want the group to speak more, or less, French than we did?

Would the exchange be useful and pleasant for a student who didn't speak French? Explain.

Presentation:

     What was the title of your presentation?

     Describe the group to which you gave it:

     About how many people were in that group?

     Describe how it went—and any supplementary materials you had:

What questions did people ask you?

Did you speak French or English?

Did your audience speak French or English?

Planned program:

Did you have enough free time in Geneva? Too much? If not enough, what did you   want to do that you didn't have time to do?

Describe how you spent the vacation week:

Saturday:

Sunday:

Monday:

Tuesday:

Wednesday:

Thursday:

Friday:

Saturday:

Sunday:

Please rate each of the following activities from 1 (low) to 10 (couldn't be better). If 3 or lower, or 7 or higher, please explain your answer, based on interest and usefulness.

_____ Reception with "petits tambours de Meyrin"

_____ Cross country ski trip

_____ M. Troesch's slide presentation on Switzerland

_____ Lunch at DeSaussure

_____ Tour of Old City

_____ McDonald's

_____ Red Cross

_____ Raclette/entertainment

_____ Cave du Mandement

_____ Rolex

_____ Wendy's

_____ Rally in Old City

How much of the rally did you complete? _____%

How long did it take your group? _____ hours

_____ Potluck supper

_____ Nestlé factory

_____ Cheese factory

_____ Château at Gruyère

_____ Berne

_____ Bank (stock exchange, currency exchange, lunch)

_____ Apéritif for parents

_____ Disco/soirée d'adieux

Journal:

When did you start writing in your journal?

How often did you write in it?

Describe the sort of thing you wrote.

Was the journal useful to you? Why, or why not?

General evaluation:

Describe the Cassidys' relationship with you:

How could the Cassidys have made your experience easier or more enjoyable?

Did you feel that the Cassidys treated the group (as a whole) fairly?

Did they treat individuals within the group fairly?

What did you learn about yourself during the trip?

Do you want to go back to Switzerland? Why or why not?

Are you looking forward to the arrival of the Swiss in July? Why or why not?

Would you recommend the exchange to a friend? Why or why not?

Do you have suggestions for improving the exchange? Please list them:

Give the exchange a grade (A+-F): _____

Give yourself a grade for the trip (based on how much you put into it and how much you got out of it): _____

Formal test

Journals and self-evaluations may not be enough for you or for the powers that be at school, so you may want to administer a formal test. If you decide to test the students on specific information, administering the test before they begin their orientation will show you how much they already know; it will also give the students a clear idea of the kinds of things you expect them to learn during the trip.

The test, which you'll probably have to design yourself to fit your trip, can measure cultural information, language comprehension, or even spoken language. It can be utterly objective (multiple-choice or fill-ins), moderately open-ended (short answers) or quite open-ended (questions asking for analysis or individual opinion); it can be in writing or it can be partly oral, though, of course, a test of spoken language will require an oral component, either live or on tape.

Formal self-evaluation

The Experiment in International Living has a formal self-evaluation procedure, based on a form called the Y.O.G.A. (Your Objectives, Goals, and Assessments). Students fill out the form at the beginning of their intensive language training, at the end of that training, and at the end of their stay abroad. I adapted the form for use with my students; I print the adaptation with the kind permission of the Experiment in International Living. You could adapt the form to your students' needs.

SELF-EVALUATION—FORMAL

Please rate yourself on a scale of 1-5 in the following aspects of LISTENING AND SPEAKING French. You will be asked to rate yourself again at the end of the exchange program.

The rating system is as follows:

1—never tried

2—can understand and make myself understood with great difficulty; I don't really know the structures or vocabulary but fake it a little.

3—I can understand and make myself understood with difficulty. I know what the structures and vocabulary are, but can't use them easily.

4—I can speak and understand fairly smoothly. I still make some mistakes, but I can express myself without difficulty.

5—I can speak and understand just as if I were speaking English.

I. Grammar	1	2	3	4	5

1. Forms of the present tense of verbs, both regular and irregular.
2. Forms of the imperfect and its use (I was going to . . . I *used* to do something)
3. Forms of the *passé composé*
4. Other compound tenses (I would have gone, I will have been, I had been, etc.)
5. Forms of the *futur proche* (I'm going to do something . . .)
6. Forms of the future
7. Forms of the conditional (I would . . .)
8. Direct and indirect object pronouns *(le, les, lui, me, te, etc.)*
9. Interrogatives: question words and the word order that follows them
10. Possessive adjectives and pronouns (my, mine; your, yours; etc.)
11. Numbers 1-1,000,000 and ordinals (third, twenty-fifth, hundred and twenty-fifth)

II. Actual communication in French	1	2	3	4	5

1. Greetings and polite expressions; introductions, formal and informal
2. Describing your family
3. Describing your house, the different rooms in it, the furniture, etc.
4. Telling time and using expressions of time ("a year ago," "since yesterday," "in these months," etc.)
5. Describing your town, its population, location, layout, main industries, shops, etc.
6. Describing your school, your courses, teams, extra-curricular activities
7. Describing Vermont, its geography, history, political system, industries
8. Describing the U.S. (see Vermont, above)
9. Using a telephone in French

	1	2	3	4	5

10. Using public transportation (bus, train, subway) in French
11. Discussing food (ordering a simple meal in a restaurant, or talking about food with your host family)
12. Discussing health, describing your symptoms if you are not feeling well
13. Watching TV, listening to the radio, reading newspapers, seeing movies

III. Culture	1	2	3

Switzerland

How much do you know about these aspects of Switzerland? Please rate yourself on a scale of 0-2, as follows: **0**—no knowledge at all; **1**—I have a vague impression, but can't speak knowledgeably; **2**—I have solid knowledge, from reading or from experience or from being told by a Swiss.

1. Swiss geography (what countries border it, what are the main cities cities and regions)
2. Swiss history
3. The present political system (how the government is organized, who leads it, what its policies are toward Europe, the U.S., the rest of the world)
4. What political or social questions are important now to the Swiss and why
5. Swiss currency (the units, their worth in terms of the U.S. dollar)
6. Geneva: its layout, how to use the transportation system
7. Geneva: its history and points of interest

There are other evaluations that can be very useful to you as leader in planning and improving your program, even though they may not measure students' progress.

Parents' evaluation

After both parts of our exchange were finished, I distributed the following questionnaire to the American parents. They were free to sign their names, and their comments, both positive and negative, were frank and therefore very helpful. Here's the form I used, which you can adapt to fit your program.

PARENTS' EVALUATION

If you can answer this questionnaire as fully and as openly as possible, it will help us with future exchanges. If you don't wish to put your name, that's fine. Please feel free to use the back of this questionnaire for more complete answers.

I. Trip to Geneva

1. Was your child adequately prepared for the whole trip?

   What preparation was most useful?

   What further preparation would have been useful to your child?

2. What did your child get out of the Paris trip?

   Was the Paris trip worth the extra time and money for your child?

   Could that part of the trip have been improved for your child?

3. I'd appreciate any comments you have on the following aspects of your child's experience abroad.

   Planned activities:

   Those he or she liked best:

   Those he or she liked least:

   Comments:

The homestay

4. The general relationship between your child and his or her partner:

   The relationship between him or her and the rest of the homestay family:

   Other comments:

Free time

5. The amount of free time your child seemed to have:

How did your child use his or her free time?

What could we (Swiss and American adults) have done to ensure that the students would all use their free time profitably?

Other comments:

Language

6. Are you satisfied with your child's progress in French?

What seemed to be the most useful aspects of the trip in improving your child's French?

Would you have been in favor of language/civilization classes (for perhaps 2 hours per day during our stay, if our other activities were adjusted to allow for them)? Why or why not?

Other comments:

II. The Swiss Visit to Brattleboro

7. Your visitor's willingness to share your family's life:

8. His or her willingness to live according to your family's rules:

9. The amount of free time in the program:

Your guest's use of the free time in program:

10. The involvement of the Swiss and American chaperones in the group's activities:

Other comments on the chaperones' relationship with the group:

11. The most negative aspect (or moment) of the Swiss stay in Brattleboro:

12. The most positive aspect (or moment) of the Swiss stay in Brattleboro:

13. Any suggestions you have for improving either side of the exchange:

Would you recommend the exchange to another family—or encourage another of your your own children to participate? Why or why not?

Name (if you like) _____

Visitors' evaluation

On the last evening of their stay in Brattleboro, we distributed a questionnaire to the Swiss visitors to find out their reactions to their experiences in their American families and to the program the families had planned for them. The questionnaire follows:

VISITORS' EVALUATION

Please respond, as completely as possible, to the following questions. You don't have to sign your name; your honest answers will help improve future exchanges.

I. Preparation

1. Why did you participate in this exchange?

2. How long have you studied English?

3. Did you have difficulty speaking English? Yes _____ No _____

   Sometimes _____ In what situation(s)? Give examples.

4. What did you do to prepare yourself for this exchange?

5. What could you have done as preparation, or what could others have done so that you'd feel more at ease and get more out of the exchange?

II. The homestay

1. Did you have to share a room? With whom?

   Was the situation bothersome?

2. Did your partner work? How many hours per day?

   Did the family make an effort to keep you busy while your counterpart worked?

   What did they do?

   Was your counterpart with you when he or she wasn't working?

3. Were you left alone at home? All the time _____ Often _____ Sometimes _____ Almost never _____

4. Did the family give you enough freedom?

5. Did you go to places outside Brattleboro with the family?

6. What percentage of the time did you speak English with the family? _____%

   With the other young people during group activities? _____%

   Are you satisfied with your progress in English?

   What helped you the most?

   Did the family help to improve your English? How?

   What would you have liked them to do?

7. Did the family willingly explain aspects of American life that you didn't understand?
   Give examples.

8. Describe your relationship with the family.

   Were there problems of communication? Describe them.

III. Activities

1. Please give a number to each activity to indicate your opinion of it: 0=very boring; 3=so-so; 5=really great).

   a. Welcome, parade of cars

   b. Welcome party with disco

   c. Visit to sugar house

   d. Visit to Sturbridge

   e. Picnic at the Wilcoxes'

   f. Visit to the School for International Training

   g. Trip to Boston

   h. Bonfire, hayride and cookout at the Evans farm

   i. Disco at Flat Street

   j. Visit to Book Press

   k. Visit to toy factory and swimming

   l. Clambake

2. Would you have participated in the exchange if there had been included in the program 2 hours of class per day (English language and American civilization)?

   Why or why not?

3. Do you have other suggestions for group activities?

IV. General

1. What's your favorite memory of your stay in Brattleboro?

2. What's your least favorite memory?

3. Would you recommend such an exchange to a friend?

   Why or why not?

Credit for you

Just as the students should get credit for the work they put into the trip and what they learn from it, you too should get what benefits you can for the untold effort that you put into it and all that you learn from it. Leading a trip will develop your organizational skills; just keeping track of all the forms is a job in itself—to say nothing of scheduling meetings, working with the travel agent on details of your travel, arranging your program with your counterpart, and supervising fund-raising activities.

ACADEMIC CREDIT. You can seek academic credit from an educational institution, either incorporating the trip in an existing course, or developing an independent project for credit. Though you'll probably have to pay tuition to the institution for the credits you receive, the tuition payments may at least be tax deductible (see "Tax deductions," below).

Consult a continuing-education specialist or a faculty member in an appropriate department at the college or university for guidelines on how to proceed. Before you actually propose to receive academic credit for the trip, you should consider what you'll produce as documentation of your work. Some possibilities:

- a journal or narrative paper focusing on your administrative tasks and what you learn from them, your dealings with the students and what you learn from them, or cross-cultural aspects of the trip—or some combination of these ideas;

- a collection of materials that you find or create as you work with the students. Such a collection could be invaluable to another teacher planning a trip to the same destination;

- a formal study of some aspect of the trip; for example, you could find out just what the students learned in a given area during the trip—or what they failed to learn; you could design pre- and post-tests to measure their learning. Or you could see whether the trip affects the attitudes (toward the subject matter or the host country) of the participants in the trip or even of other students in the school who don't go on the trip themselves.

Goddard College offers graduate credit to educators for independent study incorporating travel. It's not necessary to matriculate at Goddard, or to spend time on its campus, to take this course. The address:

Goddard College
Travel for Academic Growth
Plainfield, Vermont 05667
Att: James Galloway, Faculty/Director
Phone: (802) 454-7835 or 454-8311

RECERTIFICATION CREDITS. In a few states you can get credits toward recertification for extra projects connected with your teaching but above and beyond the normal demands of your job, even if the projects don't earn formal academic credit. For details, check with the superintendent or the certification officer in the district or in the state education department.

TAX DEDUCTIONS. It pays to keep detailed records of *all* your expenses connected with the trip (e.g., materials you buy, any long-distance calls you make on your home phone, meals and transportation that you pay for when you're abroad). Presumably the students will be paying for your airfare, your hotel, and similar large items, but there may be smaller expenses that you'll have to pay for out of your own pocket. If you keep and file your receipts, you may be able to deduct these expenses from your taxes; though at present (1988) the tax laws disallow deductions for educational travel *as such*, you may be able to claim any tuition you pay and certain expenses as an educational expense if your receive academic credit for some aspect of the experience. Since both the tax laws and the courts' interpretations of them can change every year, it's wise to consult an accountant or a current, comprehensive tax guide before you claim these deductions.

OTHER CREDIT. The most important credit you'll get for all your work is the kind that is never documented anywhere. It's the credit that students, or their families, give you—sometimes years later—for sharing an experience that changed their lives. There's a special bond that is obvious when you see them again; surprising numbers of them will become your friends. Just as the students get out of their travel what they put into it, you will reap rich rewards from everything that you put into it for them and with them. That's why, a year or two or three later, you may find youself with another group, on your way again.

Other Intercultural Texts and Resources from Pro Lingua Associates

Beyond the Language Classroom
A Guide for Teachers

by Maggie Brown Cassidy, Albert Lynch, Elizabeth Tannenbaum, and Larraine Wright. Alvino E. Fantini, editor.

If you are taking students abroad or planning a visit from exchange students, this guide explains how to identify and use language/culture resources to enrich your students' experience and to provide opportunities for experiential language learning. It explores three significant areas: 1. using foreign exchange students as resources (a growing interest in American schools); 2. using American students returning from overseas as resources; and 3. finding and using other resources in the community. The goal is to move students toward communicative competence and to help them form intercultural friendships founded on mutual respect and understanding.

Living in France, Germany, Japan, Italy, Great Britain, Mexico, or the United States

The seven handbooks in this series are ideal handouts for the students you are taking abroad to these countries. Each book 1. describes point-by-point how to meet your survival needs upon arrival (food, transportation, money, safety, etc.); 2. looks at important cultural features which may differ significantly from your own; and 3. provides an overview of the nation's history, geography, peoples, and government. The books are inexpensive, easy to use during orientation, and then easy to carry along. Handbooks on other countries are planned.

Experiential Language Teaching Techniques

by Michael Jerald and Raymond C. Clark. If you are teaching French in France, Spanish in Spain, or ESL anywhere where there is an English speaking community, these carefully structured out-of-class activities will bring your students' language learning to life, raising their motivation and sense of achievement. Step by step the language learner is brought into contact with the community, and assignment after fun assignment they build their communicative competence the natural way. This is an ideal handbook for you if you will be teaching language while you are taking students abroad, anywhere, or working with exchange students in the States.

Cultural Awareness Teaching Techniques

by Jan Gaston. Whether you are planning orientation before taking students abroad, are organizing intercultural activities during your trip, or just want to raise your students' cultural awareness, the 20 conversation techniques given in this teacher's handbook will have a great impact on your teaching and on your students' interest and understanding. Each technique can be used on its own, or the 20 can be used together as a curriculum which will guide your students through 4 intercultural skill-building stages until they are able to function comfortably in other cultures, with both respect and empathy and with a strong appreciation for their own culture as well. "Every language teacher should get to know this book!"

Beyond Experience

Edited by Donald Batchelder and Elizabeth G. Warner. This classic in the field of intercultural communication and training presents a collection of articles that cover both the theoretical and practical aspects of cross-cultural orientation as it has been practiced by The Experiment in International Living, the organization which started the movement of taking students abroad for 'homestays' back in the thirties. The three sections of the book focus on *ideas* for the overall design of experiential intercultural programs, *exercises* designed specifically for achieving the goals set in the first section, and methods of *assessment* to help the learner identify what still needs to be learned.

If you would like to order any of these books, or if you would like more information about them or the other language/cultural texts and teacher resources published by **Pro Lingua Associates,** *please write to us at* **15 Elm Street, Brattleboro, Vermont 05301, U.S.A.,** *or call us at* **802-257-7779.**